Dr. Janet Jones

Do Brilliantly

A2 Sociology

Rob Webb
Series Editor: Jayne de Courcy

Contents

Published by HarperCollins*Publishers* Ltd
77–85 Fulham Palace Road
London W6 8JB

www.**Collins**Education.com
On-line support for schools and colleges

First published 2002

ISBN 0 00 712423 6

British Library Cataloguing in Publication Data
A catalogue record for this book is available from the British Library.

Edited by Steve Attmore
Production by Kathryn Botterill
Book design by Gecko Ltd
Cover design by Susi Martin-Taylor
Printed and bound by Scotprint

Acknowledgements
The Author and Publishers are grateful to the following for permission to reproduce copyright material:

AQA Specimen examination papers are reproduced by permission of the Assessment and Qualifications Alliance. The author is responsible for the possible answers/solutions and the commentaries. They may not constitute the only possible solutions.
Murray Morison, *Methods in Sociology* published by Longman in 1986; extract from D. Mason, *Race and Ethnicity in Modern Britain* (1995) by permission of Oxford University Press;
N. Abercrombie et al, *Contemporary British Society* 2nd edition, Polity Press, 1994

Every effort has been made to contact the holders of copyright material, but if any have been inadvertently overlooked, the Publishers will be pleased to make the necessary arrangements at the first opportunity.

Photographs
The publishers would like to thank the following for permission to reproduce photographs:
(c) Credit: Sally Greenhill, Sally & Richard Greenhill Photo Library page 15;
Telegraph Colour Library page 55.

Illustrations
Roger Penwill, Gecko Ltd

You might also like to visit:
www.**fire**and**water**.com
The book lover's website

How this book will help you

by Rob Webb

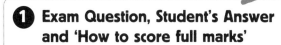

Exam practice – how to answer questions better

This book will help you to improve your performance in your A2 Sociology exams.

Every year I mark exam papers where students don't use the information that they've learnt as effectively as they could. This means they don't get the grade they're capable of achieving.

To get a high grade in A2 Sociology you need a good grasp of the subject matter **and good exam technique**. Your textbook and your class notes can help you develop your knowledge and understanding. **This book will help you improve your exam technique, so that you can make the most effective use of what you know.**

Each chapter in the book is broken down into four separate elements, aimed at giving you the guidance and practice you need to improve your exam technique:

❶ Exam Question, Student's Answer and 'How to score full marks'

Each chapter starts with an exam question of the sort you will find on a real A2 Sociology paper. This is followed by a typical student's answer.

The 'How to score full marks' sections show you where and how the student's answers could be improved, e.g. by explaining what the question is asking for, by pointing out missing knowledge etc. **This means that when you meet these sorts of questions in your exam, you will know how to tackle them successfully.**

I have also written a paragraph-by-paragraph commentary alongside the student's answer, pointing out what is good, what is not so good, and what is missing. **This makes it clear what examiners such as myself are looking for in order to award marks.**

❷ 'Don't forget ...' boxes

These boxes highlight some of the most common mistakes I see every year in students' exam papers. These include both sociological errors (such as writing about the wrong aspect of a topic) and faulty exam technique.

When you're doing last minute revision, you can quickly read through these boxes. It's also worth looking at the boxes in chapters covering topics that you *haven't* studied, because these often contain useful general points that may apply to your topics too.

❸ 'Key points to remember'

Every chapter has a 'Key points to remember' page, giving you a quick overview of the topic as a whole and listing the most important points that you will need to cover when revising that topic. But remember – a book of this size can't hope to cover all the detailed sociological information you need for your exams – that's what your textbook and class notes are for!

❹ Questions to try, Answers and Examiner's hints and comments

Each chapter ends with **a full exam question for you to try answering**. Don't cheat! Sit down and try to answer it as if you were in an exam. Try to remember all that you've read in the chapter and put it into practice here. To help you, **I've included a couple of 'Examiner's hints' giving you some tips on how to tackle the essay questions.**

When you've written your answer, check it through and make any additions or alterations, then turn to the back of the book. There you'll find an answer to the question you've just done. This answer is of a very good 'A' grade standard. **I've added my 'Examiner's comments' to show you exactly why it's such a good answer.**

Compare your answer with the answer given. If you feel that yours wasn't as good, **you can use the one given and my comments on it to help you decide which aspects of your answer you could improve on.**

The topics covered by your specification

You are probably following the **AQA specification**, which is the one most students sit. It has six topics, organised into **three modules**. Most of these topics also appear on the OCR specification for AS or A2 Sociology, which is the other exam board for Sociology. The table below shows how this book covers the topics for both the AQA and OCR exams:

AQA topics	Chapter in this book	OCR topics
Power & Politics (Module 4)	1	Protest & Social Movements (Module 5)*
Religion (Module 4)	2	Religion (Module 2)*
World Sociology (Module 4)	3	*No equivalent topic*
Theory & Methods (Module 5)	4	Applied Sociological Research Skills (Module 6)
Crime & Deviance (Module 6)	5	Crime & Deviance (Module 5)
Stratification & Differentiation (Module 6)	6	*part of* Social Inequality & Difference (Module 8)

* indicates an AS topic in the OCR specification.

What you have to study

For A2 Sociology, you have to sit three exam papers or 'units'. Each unit examines a module of study. (A module is what you study; a unit is the exam paper you take on that module.) For AQA, these modules are:

4 Power & Politics; Religion; World Sociology
5 Theory & Methods
6 Crime & Deviance; Stratification & Differentiation

(Note: modules 1, 2 and 3 are the AS modules; modules 4, 5 and 6 are the A2 modules.)

You must study at least one topic from each module and answer a question on it in the exam paper. So, for example, you could study and answer a question on Religion in unit 4, and on Crime & Deviance in unit 6. For the unit 5 written exam, there is only one topic – Theory & Methods – so if you are taking this exam, then obviously this is what you must study! However, for unit 5, your school or college may decide to enter you for the Coursework option instead of the written exam. You should check with your teacher about this.

For OCR A2 Sociology, the topics are allocated differently to the different modules and the modules follow a slightly different numbering system. These are as follows:

5 Power & Control (one topic from Crime & Deviance, Education, Health, Popular Culture, Social Policy & Welfare, Protest & Social Movements)
6 Applied Sociological Research Skills
7 Personal Study (coursework option instead of Module 6)
8 Social Inequality & Difference

The questions in this book are written in the same style as the **AQA exam questions**. However, as there are similarities between AQA and OCR questions, **this book will help you prepare for either AQA or OCR exams**.

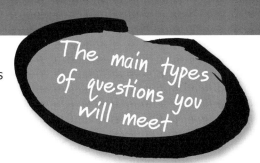
The main types of questions you will meet

All three AQA A2 exam papers have the following features: data-response Items; shorter questions and essay questions.

Data-response Items

Sometimes called stimulus-response Items, **these are pieces of material for you to use in answering part or parts of the question**. They may be extracts of text from Sociology books (including textbooks), magazines and newspaper articles. They may be tables of figures, charts, graphs, diagrams or even photographs. The important thing to remember is that these Items are there to help you answer the questions. In fact, **many of the questions actually instruct you to use the Items – so unless you want to throw marks away, make sure you do use them!**

Shorter questions

A typical AQA A2 unit is marked out of a total of 60 marks. Shorter questions appear on all three A2 units, and in each case they are **worth a total of 20 of the 60 marks**. On unit 5 (Theory & Methods), they often take the form of **four** questions (worth 2, 4, 6 and 8 marks). On units 4 and 6, they often take the form of **two** questions (worth 8 and 12 marks).

The shortest of these may ask you to **define or explain the meaning of a key sociological concept**. Others may ask you to **identify and analyse or discuss two or more factors, reasons, criticisms, etc. connected with the topic**. Many of these shorter questions are linked to the Items – for example, you may be asked to give a reason for a point made in the Item – but some of them may simply test the knowledge that you bring to the exam. Some of the questions, such as those worth 8–12 marks, may ask you to **discuss or examine some of the issues or problems connected with a topic**. You would be expected to write two or more full paragraphs for such questions (and more for a 12-mark question).

Essay questions

All three AQA A2 units require you to answer one essay question. In each case, the essay is **worth 40 marks – two-thirds of the total 60 marks for that unit**. On unit 4, once you have chosen your topic (e.g. Religion), you will have a choice of one essay question from two. Unit 5 (Theory & Methods) also has a choice of one essay from two. On Unit 6 (Crime & Deviance or Stratification & Differentiation), you must answer a compulsory essay question on your chosen topic.

In all cases, you should spend some time making a plan. Study the question. The wording of an essay question needs particular attention, because it is inviting you to write at length about something and so you need to think about all the possible issues and aspects that it raises. Look at the command word (see 'Exam Tips' on page 6). Brainstorm and make a list (or diagram) of the main theories, studies, facts, concepts, examples, etc. that you think may be relevant. Decide what is the best order in which to present your material and how to link what you know to what the question is asking for. **As you write your answer, keep referring back both to your plan and to the wording of the question** to check you're still answering it! Write an introduction and a conclusion.

OCR questions

OCR A2 exam questions are generally similar to AQA questions: there are data-response Items, data-response questions and essays. However, unit 5 (Power & Control) has only essay questions and is marked out of 60, while the other two involve Items and data-response questions. Of these two, unit 6 (Applied Sociological Research Skills) is marked out of 90, and unit 8 (Social Inequality & Difference) is marked out of 120.

Synoptic assessment

Synoptic assessment is a key feature of exams in all A level subjects. **It is a way of testing your knowledge and understanding of the subject as a whole**, rather than just of the particular 'chunks' of it that are examined in each unit.

In AQA A level Sociology, **this is done in unit 6 – the final A2 unit**. For example, if you have studied Crime & Deviance in module 6, the exam will test not only what you know about crime and deviance, but also your understanding of **the links** between crime and deviance and **other topics that you have studied at both AS and A2**. (For OCR, the synoptic unit is unit 8 – Social Inequality & Difference.)

The synoptic unit is also worth slightly more than the other A2 units in terms of your final result: 20 per cent of the total marks for your A level come from this paper, as against only 15 per cent for each of the other two A2 units.

To help you make the links, I have included a special synoptic section in chapters 5 and 6. This looks at some of the links between the two AQA unit 6 topics and every one of the other 11 topics covered at AS and A2.

Exam Tips

- **Make a brief plan before writing.** Stick to it and refer back to it throughout when writing your answer.
- **Use the Items.** They're there to help you and, if you don't use them when the question tells you to, you'll be throwing away marks. To make the most of the Items, read them through several times, picking out or underlining key points and letting your mind digest them. Think how they link up with your own knowledge.
- **Use examples** – from sociological studies, the news, coursework if you're doing it, the media/fiction, your knowledge of other subjects – in fact from anywhere, so long as you can show how and why they're relevant to the question.
- **Allocate your time sensibly.** There's no point spending half your exam time answering a question that's only worth a fifth of the marks – or a fifth of your time answering a question worth a half of the total marks! Use the marks available as a rough guide to how much to write.
- **Know the meaning of the key command words.** These include:
  - **'Identify...'** Here you must show that you can recognise an argument, example, idea, fact, viewpoint, reason, criticism, etc. (depending on what the question is about). Often the question will ask you to develop the point you have identified, by asking you to 'briefly discuss' or 'briefly explain' it.
  - **'Explain...'** In an essay, you must show a detailed knowledge and understanding of something, and apply it in a relevant way to the question. This often implies that you need to know **'why'** as well.
  - **'Examine...'** You must consider in detail the relevant information (evidence, arguments, concepts, views, etc.). Sometimes a question may ask you only to examine the evidence for and/or against, rather than the arguments (or vice versa).
  - **'Discuss/Critically discuss...'** Present the different positions or views in an argument and arrive at a conclusion based on your discussion.
  - **'Using material from Item A...'** You must select relevant information from the Item and use it to help answer the question. It's perfectly OK to quote from the Item, or to paraphrase it in your own words (at least this shows you've read it!), but you must also interpret and use the information in ways that are relevant to the question, e.g. by building on it or linking it to some of your own knowledge. Remember – there may well be more than one point you could use from the Item.
  - **'Assess...'** Here you must show the skill of **evaluation**, weighing up arguments and/or evidence for and against, considering different viewpoints, and drawing an appropriate conclusion based on what you have said earlier. Sometimes you may be asked to assess the strengths and limitations, or the advantages and disadvantages – usually of a particular view, theory, study, method and so on. Look at both sides and draw a conclusion as to whether one side outweighs the other, based on your arguments and evidence for each.

1 Power and Politics

Part One

Item A

Pluralists see power as dispersed throughout society, with many different groups competing to affect decisions in their favour. No single group or class is able to dominate the decision-making process, and as the different groups compete for influence, the state acts as a neutral arbiter [independent judge]. Because politicians need to get elected, they cannot afford to ignore public opinion and so must appeal to 5 many different sections of the electorate to win their vote, and political parties act as vehicles for grouping together many different interests. However, both Marxists and elite theorists have criticised pluralists for having a naïve view of the state and politics.

1 (a) Identify and briefly describe **two** similarities between the views of Marxists and elite theorists on the distribution of power **(Item A, lines 7–8)**.

[8 marks]

(b) Using material from **Item A** and elsewhere, briefly examine some of the criticisms of the pluralist view of the state and politics.

[12 marks]

Part Two

Answer **one** question from this Part.

2 Assess the view that social class has ceased to be the most important factor influencing political participation in Britain today.

[40 marks]

3 Assess sociological explanations of the role of the mass media in the political process.

[40 marks]

1 (a) Identify and briefly describe **two** similarities between the views of Marxists and elite theorists on the distribution of power **(Item A, lines 7–8)**.

[8 marks]

VAL'S ANSWER

One similarity between elite theorists and Marxists is that they both believe that power is concentrated in the hands of a few people — an elite that dominates society. For example, the political elite generally tend to come from a fairly privileged minority background. So too do the judges, top civil servants etc. Marxists refer to the power group as the ruling class, the capitalist class that owns the factories, land etc. This wealth enables them to dominate politics and decision making. In both theories, a minority are the true rulers of society.

On the other hand, they disagree about where this power comes from. Elite theorists like Pareto believe in 'lions' and 'foxes' — that is, different kinds of elites based on their psychological make-up (lions are bold, ruthless etc. and seize power, whereas foxes are cunning and manipulate people or make alliances to hold on to power). Marxists believe that elite power comes from capitalism, i.e. from ownership of wealth or means of production.

Another similarity is that they (Marxists and elite theorists) both think that those who have the power (the elite) use it to benefit themselves whereas pluralists think power is a variable sum where everyone gets something.

6/8

Val correctly points out that both types of theorist see power as concentrated in the hands of a minority – whether an 'elite' as elite theorists argue, or a 'ruling class' as Marxists believe. She gives a satisfactory description as well.

It's not clear what Val's up to here. She seems to have switched to automatic and is telling us how Marxism and elite theory *differ* – but the question only asks for *similarities*.

Good point identified. Both types of theorist see the ruling group as using power in their own self-interest – but Val needs to develop the point.

How to score full marks

Answer the question – don't go off the subject as Val does in her second paragraph. If you're asked for similarities, don't bother with differences (and vice versa). What Val wrote was interesting and accurate, but irrelevant to the question. It gained her no marks! Examiners are impressed when you show your knowledge – but only when it actually helps to answer the question.

On these 'identify and briefly describe…' questions, make sure that you **enlarge on the point that you have identified**. Val does this well with her first point, but the second one (her last paragraph) remains undeveloped. For example, you could talk about how Marxists see laws that are passed as being **biased in favour of big business**.

(b) Using material from **Item A** and elsewhere, briefly examine some of the criticisms of the pluralist view of the state and politics.

[12 marks]

VAL'S ANSWER

As Item A shows, pluralists believe that the state is neutral, like a referee. It does not take sides when there is a conflict between different groups, so it is not controlled by one particular section. Pluralists such as Dahl argue that no one group always gets its own way. In a study of local decision making in New Haven (USA) he looked at who participated in decision making in different areas such as education and urban redevelopment. He found that a lot of different groups were involved, but mostly only in one issue. So no one group took all the decisions, instead a lot had some say and the decisions that were reached were often a compromise between different groups and their interests.

> This is quite a good description of Dahl and shows understanding of the pluralist view, but Val has not referred to any criticisms yet.

One criticism of Dahl's approach to power is that he only looks at decisions and who is involved in taking them. Lukes argues that power has three faces, and that Dahl has only considered one of them. The other two are non-decision making or agenda setting, and ideology, but pluralists neglect these faces of power and only look at the most obvious aspect of it.

> Val has begun to look at criticisms, but has not made herself very clear – what *are* agenda setting and ideology?

Also although, as pluralists say, there are different groups in society competing for influence, some of them are stronger than others and more likely to get their way. The pluralists don't give enough attention to this. For example, wealthy groups like business can 'buy' more influence, whether by bribery at times, or by being able to fund campaigns, sponsor MPs etc. On the other hand, poor groups (e.g. old age pensioners or lone parents) are not likely to have much clout, and might also lack skills needed for politics (e.g. confidence, knowledge).

> A good point here, with some relevant examples. Maybe she could give it some theoretical context, though.

Critics argue, as it says in Item A, that pluralists are naïve. Some pluralists respond by combining their ideas with elite theory ideas to develop elite pluralism. This type of pluralism is more realistic because it recognises that not all groups have equal power — e.g. some groups are insider groups (e.g. business) and have more say than outsider groups (e.g. CND, animal liberation) because the 'establishment' (civil servants etc.) trust them more, share the same background and values etc. This is more realistic, but less pluralist. So overall it is true to say that pluralism has a naïve view of politics.

> A relevant point that some of pluralism's weaknesses can be overcome to some extent by taking on board other perspectives, such as elite theory. Some useful examples, too.

7/12

 Although you need to know what pluralists argue, your main focus should be on the **criticisms** of their views. Val wastes time at the beginning setting out the pluralist view at some length.

 Val rightly draws attention to the fact that pluralists only look at one 'face' of power, but she needs to explain more clearly what the other faces – agenda setting and ideology – actually are. **Agenda setting** (or 'non-decision making') is about the ability of some groups to prevent certain issues ever getting discussed. Powerful groups can also impose their **ideology** on others to persuade them that they share the same goals and interests (e.g. that decisions benefiting the rich will also benefit the poor).

 Val makes some useful points, but there isn't much **theory** in her answer. You could improve on it by bringing in **Marxist or other theories** of the nature and distribution of power. One way to do this would be to look at the **nature of democracy** from different standpoints. The basic question here is whether democracy – rule by and for the majority – is **real** (as pluralists argue) or an **illusion** cloaking the interests of the powerful (as Marxists and elite theorists claim).

 You could make more reference to Item A, including **the role of pressure groups and parties**. These are key features of the democratic process for pluralists, since they are seen as voicing and aggregating (grouping together) the interests of different sections of the population so that government can take them on board in decision making. But **New Right critics** argue that this brings **government overload** – because they desire re-election, governments try to meet everyone's needs, usually by spending more money, thereby pushing up taxes and damaging the economy.

Don't forget ...

When asked to examine criticisms of a theory or viewpoint, although you may need to describe the theory **briefly**, your main focus has to be on **criticising** it rather than simply stating what it says.

'Criticisms' is plural – so try to deal with at least three or four main points. When 'examining' them, you need to spell things out – e.g. give relevant examples, or use other theories to give your points context.

2 Assess the view that social class has ceased to be the most important factor influencing political participation in Britain today.

[40 marks]

VAL'S ANSWER

A reasonable start, showing awareness of sociologists' interest in this area, and of changes that have occurred – but Val over-states the case in the last sentence: many people still do vote along class lines.

Sociologists' studies of voting behaviour have traditionally been focused on the relationship between social class and voting. Pulzer argues that social class is the basis for party politics. The middle classes tend to vote Conservative and working class tend to vote Labour. However, election results indicate that people are no longer voting along class lines.

If it had not been for a larger number of working-class members voting Conservative then they would not have won the general election in 1979. This is evidence that social class is no longer the major influence on voting behaviour.

The first point is reasonable, but it doesn't necessarily mean class is not still the *major* influence – even if it is less influential than before.

Butler and Stokes examined the relationship between social class and voting and said that individuals are 'socialised into party political preferences'. For example, if a family have an 18-year-old son, his voting choice is probably going to be strongly influenced by how his mother or father vote. If they vote Labour, there is a strong likelihood that he will vote Labour too.

This shows patterns continuing between generations, but Val doesn't link political socialisation to class.

However, although voting patterns were affected by class, Butler and Stokes also found evidence of class de-alignment. They found that as early as the 1950s some middle-class voters were voting Labour and some working class would vote Conservative. Evidence against the idea that class was the most important factor in voting behaviour was already beginning to emerge.

This is better – class de-alignment is a key idea, though at this stage (the 1950s) the term 'deviant voter' was used to describe such behaviour.

The studies done by Ivor Crewe are very relevant to the issue of social class and voting behaviour. He believes that the lack of working-class solidarity is linked to the general loosening of the class structure. Crewe developed the embourgeoisement thesis. This explains the increase in working-class electors voting Conservative due to the growth of the number of affluent members of the working class. As they become more affluent (better off), this group of workers begin to aspire to the attitudes and lifestyles of the middle class. As a result of this, they are more likely to vote for a party which is able to offer them more benefits. Goldthorpe and Lockwood reject this view and argue that affluent members of the working class still vote

Some useful material here, but could do with re-organising it to get the time sequence right.

Labour. They found that more affluent workers than non-affluent workers actually voted Labour.

Crewe developed the embourgeoisement idea further and suggests that there are two sections in the working class — the traditional working class and the new working class. The traditional working class live in council houses and work in the public sector, and the new working class live in privately owned homes and work in the private sector. Crewe argued that the fragmentation of the working class had made it harder for Labour to win.

Marxists argue that everything that happens in society is affected by class, including voting behaviour. We live in a capitalist society with two classes (bourgeoisie and working class). For the capitalist bourgeoisie to continue ruling, they need the support of the majority. By using their hegemony (ruling class ideology), the capitalist class persuade many workers to vote Conservative, the more pro-capitalist party — i.e. to vote against their own class.

The evidence put forward above supports the idea of electorate volatility and shows that class is no longer the major factor influencing voting behaviour.

20/40

> **Useful material again, but Val has not actually linked this division or fragmentation to voting patterns!**

> **A useful attempt to bring in a Marxist view, but Val needs to link it to whether class *remains* the most important factor.**

> **Volatility is a useful concept, but she has not explained it.**

How to score full marks

- Val focuses solely on **voting behaviour**, but this is **not the only type of political participation**. You need to consider others – e.g. joining a pressure group or party, standing for office, taking part in campaigning, direct action. **The middle and upper classes are over-represented** among ministers, MPs, councillors, etc. of all parties. Many **working-class** people participate in politics through **trade unions**.

- **Get the time sequence right**. Questions about voting behaviour or political participation are often concerned with how far and why the patterns have changed, so it is important to **know the main changes** (e.g. who won which elections) **and the way that explanations have changed** along with the patterns. In paragraph 5 of Val's answer it might be better if she dealt with the material in chronological order: the embourgeoisement thesis first (1950s), then Goldthorpe and Lockwood's criticisms of it (1960s), and finally its revival in the 1980s.

- Make sure you **explain fully the relevance of the material you use** and show how it links to the question. For example, Val's discussion of political socialisation shows why voting patterns remain constant between generations, but she does not connect this to **class**. Likewise, in paragraph 6, she should have linked the new working class to Conservative voting. Finally, she brings in the important concept of **volatility**, but does not explain or develop it.

How to score full marks

- Val shows a rather limited range of knowledge. You should bring in other material, such as the **changing size of classes** (e.g. if the working class is getting smaller, Labour could remain a working-class party yet see its vote decline), and **party image, leadership, policies and ideology** – and the **media's presentation** of these. Norris and Evans argue that New Labour's more right-wing ideology helped it win in 1997, while King believes it was due to the Conservatives' image of incompetence. **Consumer preference or rational choice theories** stress self-interest as the key.

- Use other theories to develop **evaluation**. For example, you could **contrast** Crewe's or Robertson's views with those of Marshall *et al* or Heath *et al* on issues like the loosening of the class structure.

Don't forget ...

Most of your answer needs to be about voting, but remember to include something on **other forms of participation**.

Even if class is declining in importance, it remains significant – so **don't exaggerate** your argument by saying class is no longer important at all.

Use specific phrases to begin evaluation comments – e.g. 'This view has been criticised by ...' or 'An opposing view has been offered by ...'.

Key points to remember

The nature and distribution of power: Weber defines power as the ability to achieve one's goals against the will of others; authority is legitimate power. Conflict theorists see power as a zero sum; functionalists see it as a variable sum. **Pluralists** argue that power can be measured by who makes and benefits from decisions, but this neglects agenda setting and ideology. **Marxists** believe power comes from owning the means of production and is in the hands of the minority capitalist ruling class. Power is used to exploit the working class, and ideology is used to win hegemony – consent to capitalist rule. Inequality and exploitation will only be ended by socialist revolution. **Elite theorists** agree that power is concentrated in the hands of a minority elite who use it to benefit themselves, but they reject the possibility of an equal society. Power may be based on psychological, organisational, military or economic resources. **Pluralists** argue that power is dispersed, not concentrated, and is based on authority given to leaders through elections. Many groups have an influence and benefit from decisions, not just a minority.

Voting behaviour and political participation: Many argue that **social class** is the key to voting. Butler and Stokes saw most people voting in line with their class interests (e.g. working-class Labour), but many deviant voters voted for the 'opposite' party. As their number increased from the 1970s, the class and partisan de-alignment explanation emerged: a weakening link between class and voting, and declining loyalty to parties, resulting from new social divisions. **Rational choice** theories argue that voters are consumers who assess the 'goods' on offer and vote in their own self-interest. Norris and Evans argue that Labour's victory in 1997 was due to **Labour's ideological shift** to more right-wing policies. As loyalty to parties declines, some argue that voters are now more affected by **the media**, but evidence for this view is limited. People also participate in politics by joining parties and pressure groups, standing for election, direct action etc. In party politics, white middle-class males are over-represented, although there has been an increase in numbers of women MPs in recent years.

The role of the state: Pluralists see modern western states as genuine democracies – leaders have to respond to the needs of the majority or be removed at the next election. They argue that the state acts as a neutral referee between competing interest groups. No single group dominates the state. **Marxists** argue that the state serves the capitalist class, but its democratic appearance means that it seems to serve all classes. Marxists disagree about how autonomous (independent) the state is, but all agree that it ultimately serves capitalist interests. **Elite theorists** believe that even modern democratic states are ruled by an elite – elections at best only offer a choice of rulers from within the elite. The **New Right** favour minimum state intervention, especially in economic affairs and welfare.

Parties, movements and pressure groups: Parties seek to win power through elections. A party has a shared ideology and policies. Parties represent the public and give them a choice of policies and candidates. **Pressure groups** (PGs) do not seek to govern, but to influence government decisions (e.g. by lobbying MPs). **Promotional** PGs campaign for a cause; **protective** PGs, or interest groups, represent the interests of a particular section of society. **New social movements** are often concerned with issues of identity, the environment and rights of marginalised groups rather than traditional economic issues. They are loosely organised and often use direct action. Examples include the gay rights, ecology and women's movements.

Question to try

Part One

Item A

Traditionally, Labour has been seen as a party of the left. That is, it has been regarded as embodying a socialist political ideology that aims for a more equal or classless society based on the idea of society collectively taking responsibility for the well-being of all, for example through increased taxation of the rich to fund increased welfare spending on the poor, as well as state ownership of key industries. However, some argue that under the leadership of Tony Blair, in recent years Labour has transformed itself into 'New Labour', abandoning its traditional socialist ideology and policies and becoming a much more right-wing party, in favour of a market economy and tolerant of social inequality.

5

1 (a) Identify and briefly explain **two** reasons why some sociologists argue that an 'equal or classless society' (**Item A, lines 2–3**) is not possible.

[8 marks]

(b) Using material from **Item A** and elsewhere, briefly examine some of the reasons why parties' policies and actions are not governed solely by their ideology.

[12 marks]

Part Two

Answer **one** question from this Part.

2 'Power in modern democracies is concentrated in the hands of a minority.'
Assess the sociological arguments for and against this view.

[40 marks]

3 Assess sociological explanations of the role of pressure groups in the political process.

[40 marks]

Examiner's hints

- In question **2**, 'arguments' means you need to know some relevant theories of power. Theories seeing power as held by a minority include Marxists and elite theorists (but remember to explain the differences between these approaches). On the other side, pluralists see power as dispersed – spread among many groups. You might look also at where feminists stand on this issue.
- A good way to tackle question **3** is in terms of the role that different perspectives see pressure groups (PGs) as playing. Pluralists see PGs as vital to democracy, enabling people to participate in decision making; whereas critics often see them as undemocratic, allowing some to wield more influence than others. Remember there are different types of PG, and try to use examples of actual PGs.

Answers can be found on pages 71–75.

Part One

Item A

There are a great many different types of religious groupings. Within Christianity, for example, we find a variety of organisations, such as Roman Catholics and Anglicans, Methodists and Baptists, Jehovah's Witnesses and Pentecostalists. These groups differ in how they are organised, what they expect of their members, and what they believe, and sociologists have made various attempts to identify and classify the different types   5
of religious organisation. The earliest attempt at producing such a classification was by Ernst Troeltsch, who distinguished between two basic forms of religious organisation: the church and the sect. Since Troeltsch, sociologists have added other types such as denominations, cults and new religious movements.

Sociologists have also noted how the different types of beliefs held by religious   10
organisations tend to attract members of different social groups. For example, the poor may be attracted to an organisation that offers a justification of their *present* suffering in terms of the *later* rewards that await them in heaven.

1   (a)   Identify and briefly describe **two** differences between a church and a sect (**Item A**, **line 8**).

[8 marks]

(b)   Using material from **Item A** and elsewhere, briefly examine some of the reasons why certain types of religious beliefs appeal to members of certain social groups (**Item A**).

[12 marks]

Part Two

Answer **one** question from this Part.

2   'Religion today is not in decline; rather, religious beliefs and practices are simply undergoing change.' Assess this view in the light of sociological evidence and arguments.

[40 marks]

3   Assess the arguments and evidence for the view that in complex societies, religion is more likely to be a source of conflict and social division than of harmony and social integration.

[40 marks]

1 (a) Identify and briefly describe **two** differences between a church and a sect (**Item A, line 8**).

[8 marks]

THOMAS' ANSWER

One example of a church, in fact the one looked at by Troeltsch originally, is the Roman Catholic church, which he thought of as the ideal type or best model of a church and based his definition on it. A church according to Troeltsch has a number of characteristics. These include such things as having a full-time, trained and specialised priesthood. A church has a hierarchy of officials, and the priests are paid by the church, and their job or 'calling' is a permanent one. For example, in the Roman Catholic church, a man has to undergo a lengthy period of training in a seminary (a religious college) where he gains the knowledge and skills he needs in order to perform his religious role. Once he is trained, he is then assigned to a parish, where he is provided with a home by the church (this could be seen to be a part of his payment). If he is successful, he may rise up the hierarchy and become a bishop, archbishop, cardinal or even pope.

A second feature of a church that helps to distinguish it from a sect is that a church is universal. This means that it is open to everyone (e.g. the word 'catholic' actually means 'universal', so the Catholic church sees itself as the universal church, for everyone). On the other hand, sects are usually 'closed' in that they are not open automatically to everyone. For example, you don't really have to undergo any serious tests to join a church — churches have 'birthright membership' where an infant is baptised into being a member, obviously without even understanding the church's beliefs. In a sect, on the other hand, you have to prove you believe and are committed to the faith, so you can only become a member as an adult, when you are in a position to understand and accept the sect's teachings.

6/8

> **What happened to sects? A good account of the idea of a permanent, paid priesthood in the church, but Thomas needs to make a contrast by telling us something about leadership in sects.**

> **Good – Thomas shows a clear difference between the two types of organisation in terms of membership criteria.**

How to score full marks

- Don't get so engrossed in giving a full account of the feature (or features) of one type of organisation that you forget to **say how it differs from the other type** – as Thomas does in the first paragraph. For example, you could say that in many sects there is less division between the leaders/priests and the ordinary members (partly because of the much higher level of commitment and knowledge that sects require just to be a member in the first place) – for example, some sects have forms of 'rotating leadership' in conducting services etc.

- You could also choose to look at **other differences between churches and sects**. For example, Troeltsch argues that churches are closely linked to the state, while sects are often persecuted by the state (frequently with the backing of the church).

1 (b) Using material from **Item A** and elsewhere, briefly examine some of the reasons why certain types of religious beliefs appeal to members of certain social groups (**Item A**).

[12 marks]

THOMAS' ANSWER

As Item A says, sociologists 'have ... noted how the different types of beliefs held by religious organisations tend to attract members of different social groups'. One reason for this is hinted at in Item A, which is that religious ideas that justify why the poor suffer from deprivation, give the poor an explanation of their current status. When people look around and see that others do not suffer the same hardships, they ask 'why should I be the one to suffer when others don't?' Some religious organisations explain the suffering of the poor as a test of their faith and if they endure it they will be rewarded in heaven.

Poverty and deprivation is also a reason for the appeal of millenarian movements. These prophesy that the end of the world is near, and that the existing social order or hierarchy will be overturned or reversed when the day comes. Another reason that millenarian movements are also likely to appeal to the poor, is that the poor are often the ones most affected by social change. For example, in the Middle Ages, German peasants turned to the millenarian movement of Thomas Muntzer, who promised to create an earthly paradise. This took place at a time of war and famine, and promised a solution to their problems.

Other groups who are marginalised by social change or adversely affected by it may also turn to certain types of religious belief. The Plains Indians turned to the ghost dance religion in the late 19th century because it reaffirmed traditional ways of life (e.g. that the buffalo would return and dead Indians would come back to life), and gave believers courage to resist by telling them that the ghost dance shirt would make them immune to the white men's bullets.

However, it is not only the poor or oppressed who are attracted to certain types of belief and organisation. For example, Bryan Wilson says that the Christian Science organisation attracts a more middle class following, because it believes that evil and unhappiness are merely illusions — suffering is due to a wrong attitude or misunderstanding. Unlike sects that attract the poor, it is not interested in the afterlife, and it justifies the relatively

A good start. Thomas uses Item A appropriately and expands on the point.

A well-explained point, and a good example.

Another good example, well used to link beliefs to social groups and their situations.

More useful examples of the links between the beliefs of different religious organisations and the social 'clientele' they attract, and reasons for their appeal. No conclusion, though – it just ends.

privileged social position of its members. By contrast, Wilson studied the Elim and Pentecostal sect, which attracted manual workers in search of beliefs that would reaffirm their worthiness despite their low social status, and would give an escape from the dull routines of their lives.

9/12

How to score full marks

🎯 Thomas has written a good answer, but it needs **a brief conclusion to pull the threads together**. For example, you could use it to make explicit the main points – about the poor, about social change and marginalisation, about the better off – that Thomas makes in the main body of the answer.

🎯 **Use the Item** (the question tells you to). For example, you could do what Thomas does – look for a way to use the Item **to get yourself started**. That way you have at least made some use of it, though of course you should look for other opportunities to draw on it, too. Another way to use the Item is by thinking about **the church/sect distinction**: sects have ideas that appeal to the poor; whereas Troeltsch argues that churches are conservative – so that they attract more support from privileged groups who have most to lose from changes in the existing social structure.

🎯 **Make use of sociological theories of religion** in your answer. Thomas gives some good **evidence** and he uses it effectively, but a really good answer would bring in some sociological **arguments** as well. **Weber and Marx** are obvious candidates – Weber's ideas about a 'theodicy of disprivilege' (religions of the poor offer explanations of their misfortune) could be used, as can Marx's argument that religion supplies the oppressed with an opiate to dull the pain of their oppression, as well as justifying the privileges of the ruling class.

🎯 Thomas' sources of evidence are not the only ones. You could also use material on **new religious movements** (NRMs) to consider how far different NRMs appeal to different groups: Halevy's famous study of **Methodism** and the working class, or Niebuhr on how, as a sect becomes **upwardly mobile**, its members may modify some of the sect's beliefs to make them more 'respectable'.

Don't forget ...

When asked to 'briefly examine', it is generally a good idea to try to bring in both evidence from examples or studies, and arguments and concepts from **theories**.

Answers to 'briefly examine' questions also benefit from a **brief conclusion**.

Material that you might be familiar with from one context or question-area can often be used in another. For example, knowledge of sects can be applied to questions on types of religious organisation, secularisation, and religion and social change – amongst other topics.

2 'Religion today is not in decline; rather, religious beliefs and practices are simply undergoing change.' Assess this view in the light of sociological evidence and arguments.

[40 marks]

THOMAS' ANSWER

Religion is very difficult to define, yet any discussion depends on the definition. Different sociologists have defined it in different ways. Durkheim used an inclusive or functional definition. He defined religion by its role in society, that of creating social solidarity. A major problem with this definition is that it includes many activities such as football or political movements because they create solidarity. Weber used an exclusive or substantive definition of religion in terms of belief in the supernatural. Other sociologists focus on elements such as collective worship, an organised set of beliefs etc.

Contrary to the statement in the question, many sociologists do think that religion is declining. Bryan Wilson believes that there has been a process of secularisation — a decline in the social significance of religious belief, practice and institutions. Wilson uses several arguments to support this view. Firstly, religious practices have declined. For example, baptisms, church marriages and religious funerals — in 1950, two out of three children were baptised, but in 1970 the figure was less than half. Nowadays, only about 10–12% of people go to church. Secondly, Wilson argues that religious beliefs have declined and fewer people now believe in God, or that the bible is the word of God. He also argues that the church has lost its significance and has been replaced by the welfare state, and that it has become secularised from within.

On the other hand, the statistics that Wilson uses could be questioned. For example, about 90% of people profess a belief in God. Also, just because the church has lost some of its functions, this does not mean it has a less important role to play. Parsons, for example, argues that it has become more specialised — e.g. setting up schemes to assist the destitute, alcoholics etc.

Thomas is right that definitions are important in discussing religion, but he needs to link this to the question of change/decline.

A useful paragraph setting out some arguments against the view in the question. It would help if Thomas clarified and developed the last sentence – e.g. what does 'secularised from within' mean?

Thomas is trying to evaluate Wilson's position, but not being very clear. It might be better to challenge Wilson's use of church attendance statistics on the grounds that they don't tell us the meaning of church attendance. Is setting up schemes for the needy 'more specialised'? Some misunderstanding of Parsons here.

There never was a golden age of religion. Even in the Victorian era, less than half the population went to church and those were mainly middle class, who did so for reasons of status and respectability rather than faith.

When we look at the world, secularisation does not seem to have occurred. Northern Ireland still experiences problems because of religion and America is an advanced country but religion remains very popular there.

The most debated argument is whether religious practices have declined. Firstly how can we judge this? People don't necessarily equate church-going with belief. Also it is not possible to measure private worship. People use TV programmes to help them worship.

Many religions are increasing in numbers, such as Islam. The growth of New Religious Movements shows that religion is not declining in importance. From the 1960s, NRMs began to develop. Many of these were old religions made more 'interesting' and emphasis was placed on having a religious 'experience' rather than following tradition. Others like ISKCON were based on eastern religions, or a combination of Christian and eastern. Others included ones that emphasised improving this life instead of the next, like Scientology. Wallis identified a typology of these religions, including world rejecting (e.g. Children of God), world affirming (e.g. Scientology) and world accommodating (e.g. neo-Pentecostal).

Religious beliefs are changing. There is a spiritual supermarket in which people can pick and mix, taking different parts from different religions. The death of Princess Diana brought out mass grief and a cult of Diana developed, showing that people still have strong religious feelings.

Weber predicted that religion would decline as society became more rationalised. However, many people still believe in God, and developments like NRMs show that religion is changing rather than disappearing.

22/40

How to score full marks

- There's always a temptation to start an essay by saying 'we first have to **define what we mean by…**', in this case, religion. But it's important to get down to answering the question quickly – so **make sure that any definitions are linked to the question**. Thomas doesn't do this, but you could – by saying that Durkheim's definition makes it almost impossible for religion to decline, since it defines religion in such broad terms.

- It would be a good idea to **make a clear distinction between religious beliefs and religious practices**, and to deal with each in turn. This will help to give your answer a clear structure.

- You should look at **different kinds of religious practices** – Thomas mentions church attendance, baptisms, marriages, funerals, private/TV worship, having a religious 'experience'. Which ones are 'new' or changing? Consider **problems of measuring them** to see if they are declining, and **problems of assessing their meaning**, which Thomas briefly touches on (e.g. Victorian church-going as a way of expressing status rather than faith).

- You should also look at **religious beliefs**. Thomas' opening remarks about definitions could come in here, in discussing what should count as 'religious'. His material on NRMs could also be better used – e.g. by looking at some of his examples (Scientology, ISKCON) to ask whether they are a different type of *religious* belief, or 'not really' religious. Likewise, he mentions American religion – but you could refer to Herzberg, who argues that religion in the USA has lost its doctrinal and supernatural dimensions (and you could link this to Weber's definition given by Thomas at the beginning).

- Thomas gives us a **conclusion that links back to the question**, but it's too brief. One point you could raise in conclusion is that it's possible religion is both declining **and** changing. As secularisation theorists such as Wilson argue, the changes are actually symptoms of its decline. You should also touch on both belief and practice, since this is what the question specifies.

Don't forget ...

Different questions on religion often make use of similar material – e.g. questions on theories of religion, secularisation or religious movements can often use the same ideas and studies, but for different purposes. So make sure you know the material, **and** how it can be applied to different topics.

'Assess' questions mean you need to focus on **evaluating** – making judgements based on arguments and evidence – not just describing what sociologists have said.

Key points to remember

Theories of religion: Many early **evolutionary** theories saw religion originating in primitive people's need to explain their experiences – a 'mistaken science', destined to disappear as genuine science took over. **Functionalists** (e.g. Durkheim) see religion as performing essential functions, such as maintaining social integration through shared beliefs and rituals. **Marxists** see religion as part of the superstructure of society, shaped by the economic base; as such, it helps maintain unequal class societies and prevent change by promoting ideologies justifying inequality. It acts as 'the opium of the masses', a consolation for the suffering of the poor. **Feminists** argue that religion maintains patriarchal society, for example by portraying God as male and by supporting traditional gender roles. **Weber** has been very influential (e.g. in the idea that religious beliefs can have an independent effect on the social structure and social change).

Types of religious organisation and the relationship between organisations, beliefs and social groups: Sociologists have identified different types of religious organisations. Troeltsch distinguished between church and sect. **Churches** are large, inclusive, hierarchical, conservative organisations that support the existing social order, while **sects** are small, exclusive bodies with voluntary membership that reject the social order as corrupt. Niebuhr suggests that **denominations** share features of both churches and sects. More recently, there has been a growth in **new religious movements** (NRMs). Wallis distinguishes between world-rejecting, world-accommodating and world-affirming NRMs. He sees them as a response to aspects of modern life such as alienation and consumerism, whereas Glock and Stark see them as a response to deprivation. Wilson sees their growth as a result of secularisation rather than a denial of it. Different beliefs attract different social groups – for example, the poor may be more attracted to beliefs that promise a reward for their suffering in a new, fairer world.

Religion as a conservative force and as initiator of change: Many sociological views on the role of religion in promoting or preventing change can be linked back to general theories of religion. Thus **Marxists** see religion as a **conservative**, ideological force preventing social change by persuading the masses that their lowly position is divinely ordained and that they will be rewarded in the afterlife for accepting their lot in this world. **Feminists** regard it as legitimising patriarchy. They see the rise of religious fundamentalism (Islamic, Christian, Hindu or other) as threatening to reverse the changes that have led to greater equality for women. **Functionalists** also see religion as playing a conservative role by reinforcing the existing value system. Many religions are based on the importance of the past (e.g. ancestor worship) and by stressing the need for continuity, they are a barrier to change. **Weber**, by contrast, argues that religion can **promote change** in some circumstances – as in the case of the rise of modern capitalism, which he sees as triggered by Calvinist beliefs about thrift and hard work. Liberation theology in Latin America and the influence of the black churches in the USA and South Africa have been suggested as recent examples of religion promoting change.

Different definitions and explanations of the nature and extent of secularisation: Sociologists disagree about the precise definition of secularisation, though most would accept that it involves a decline in the influence of religion. Issues of **measurement** are very important here, because to show whether a religion's influence has declined we must be able to measure its importance both today and in the past. Evidence shows that religious **behaviour**, such as church attendance, is in decline. However, some religious practice has become more private, so cannot be measured easily. In terms of **belief,** many argue that we now hold rational scientific, rather than religious, world-views. However, many beliefs, including even a belief in science, remain based on faith rather than reason. Religious **institutions** today have less influence than in the past (e.g. in politics, education, in influencing divorce laws, shaping public opinion etc.). However, some argue that now religion is free of these roles, it is purer and that private religion is not in decline even if the influence of churches is.

Question to try

Part One

Item A

There are many definitions of religion. For example, Robertson writes that religion 'refers to the existence of supernatural beings which have a governing effect on life'.

Many sociologists have been interested in the functions that religion performs for individuals and for society. For example, many 19th-century evolutionist writers argued that religion originated to meet the needs of primitive people. Thus Tylor   5
argued that religion – and especially the idea of the soul or spirit – came into being to explain events and experiences that were otherwise inexplicable, such as dreams, visions and death.

While Tylor and others focused on religious beliefs, a different approach to religion has focused on people's behaviour. For example, some sociologists have used statistics on   10
religious practices such as church attendance and participation in rituals like baptism to measure religiosity.

1 **(a)** Identify and briefly explain **two** problems in using 'statistics on religious practices … to measure religiosity' (**Item A, lines 10–12**).

[8 marks]

(b) Using material from **Item A** and elsewhere, briefly examine some of the problems in defining religion.

[12 marks]

Part Two

Answer **one** question from this Part.

2 Assess the view that religion can act as a powerful force for social change.

[40 marks]

3 Assess different explanations of the growth of new religious movements in today's society.

[40 marks]

Examiner's hints
- In response to question **2**, Weber's study of Protestantism and capitalism is a good basis for your answer, but you can use many other examples of religion and change from around the world (Iran, South Africa, Northern Ireland etc.) and different times. You can also use Marxist and/or functionalist views on the role of religion.
- For question **3**, though you need to know about different types and classifications of NRMs, don't get bogged down in lengthy descriptions of these types. Focus on explanations instead – such as deprivation, dislocation, rationalisation etc. Secularisation comes in too (e.g. the decline of mainstream religion gives opportunities for new types to emerge).

Answers can be found on pages 76–80.

Part One

Item A

Modernisation theorists argue that cultural factors in general, and education in particular, play a key role in development. Education is seen as *the* major means of achieving development, both at the level of society and at that of the individual. For example, education provides the necessary quantities of skilled labour required for development: literate administrators and clerical workers, technically competent peasant farmers, and 5 skilled industrial workers familiar with the latest production techniques. And as in the West, so too in the Third World itself, education is widely seen as the only real means of individual advancement and social and geographical mobility. Qualifications can be used as a way of escaping the poverty of rural life or of getting a clerical job in a government office. 10

1 (a) Identify and briefly explain **two** other ways in which education may play a role in development in Third World societies, **apart from** those referred to in **Item A.**

[8 marks]

(b) Briefly examine some of the criticisms of the role of education in Third World societies as described in **Item A**.

[12 marks]

Part Two

Answer **one** question from this Part.

2 Assess the arguments and evidence for and against the view that foreign aid is an obstacle to the development of Third World countries.

[40 marks]

3 Assess the problems faced by sociologists in trying to define and measure 'development'.

[40 marks]

1 (a) Identify and briefly explain **two** other ways in which education may play a role in development in Third World societies, **apart from** those referred to in **Item A.**

[8 marks]

CLAIRE'S ANSWER

Item A shows how education can play a vital economic function in developing countries by providing technically competent farmers, skilled industrial workers etc. These are needed for the economy to grow. Functionalists call this 'human capital'. By investing in humans by educating them, you provide the economy with the means to grow. For instance, farmers who are educated will be able to read about new seeds, fertilisers, agricultural machinery and so on and they can then apply this newly acquired knowledge to raise their productivity and their output.

However, there are other functions education performs for development in Third World countries. For example, it plays a political role (also called social cohesion). By teaching everybody the same things, it creates unity in society.

Education also plays a function by shaping personalities in ways that help a society to develop. This is a cultural and psychological function. Functionalists argue that to modernise you need to have 'modern personality-types'. For example, individuals must be able to accept and cope with change, not just always expect to do things in the same old traditional ways, otherwise new knowledge, techniques etc. will not get adopted and the country will stagnate. And they must want to become upwardly mobile as individuals. Education does this by stressing individual achievement and reward and by freeing people from superstition and the idea that tradition is always best.

6/8

How to score full marks

Watch out for questions that tell you to explain **other ways... *apart from* those in the Item**. Claire's first paragraph is wasted because it's all based on Item A. Tackle this kind of question by making a list of all the 'ways' you can think of, then go through the Item, underline the 'ways' mentioned in it and delete from your list the ones you find. Then choose the two ways you know most about and explain these clearly.

Make sure you **give a good, clear explanation** when asked for one. Claire **identifies two** other ways – creating social cohesion and modern personality-types – **but she only really explains the second one** so she only gets two marks not four for the first way. You could explain her first point by saying that education teaches to diverse groups such things as shared traditions, culture, perhaps language, thereby helping to weld them into a single nation.

1 (b) Briefly examine some of the criticisms of the role of education in Third World societies as described in **Item A**.

[12 marks]

CLAIRE'S ANSWER

According to Item A, education has a very positive function in development by equipping people with necessary knowledge and skills so they can be more productive, such as skilled industrial workers who know the latest techniques and machinery. This will enable them to compete with the West more successfully and this will lead to rising living standards. Also, Item A shows how education is 'the only real means of individual advancement and social and geographical mobility'. This means that if you get good educational qualifications, you can use them to escape rural poverty (in Third World countries the rural areas are usually poorer than the towns) and get a good job, e.g. as a civil servant.

One criticism of the role of education in the Third World is that if individuals in rural areas get educated, they just use their educational qualifications to escape from rural poverty. This is fine for the individuals with the qualifications, but what about those left behind?

Another problem is what kind of education they are actually getting. If it were like Item A is suggesting, that is an education that equips people with the latest knowledge about agricultural equipment, techniques etc., then it probably would be very useful. But a lot of the knowledge taught in education isn't like this. Instead money gets spent on setting up universities teaching philosophy, sociology etc., instead of more practical subjects that could actually help people develop the country.

Also, a lot of people don't really have access to education in Third World countries, especially in rural areas, so it's not going to help many people escape poverty anyway. Also, a lot of the illiterate are girls/women, so education is just another way that females lose out, because men exclude them from schooling.

5/12

Claire *interprets* what Item A is saying quite well, but the question asks her to examine *criticisms* of this kind of view, so she needs to bring these in early on.

A good point – but *what about* 'those left behind'? Claire needs to develop this idea further, bringing in some sociological *explanation*.

Another good point – much Third World education isn't useful to development. But again, Claire needs to look at *reasons and explanations* for this.

Good points about unequal access to education for rural populations and females. How might sociologists *explain* these inequalities? Also, the answer ends abruptly – why no conclusion?

The question asks you to 'briefly examine some of the **criticisms**'. You need to get down to these quickly – unlike Claire, who spends over a third of her answer (the whole of paragraph one) **describing** the view of education in the Item **without criticising** it. Although she later criticises the points she has drawn from the Item, Claire could have been much briefer in her summary of these initial points.

Claire eventually makes several good critical points, but you need to develop them by bringing in some **sociological explanations**. **Item A gives a clue** as to how you could do this, with its reference to **modernisation theorists**. You could build a good answer around the criticisms of their views on education that have been made by other rival theories or perspectives. For example, **feminists** argue that 'development' doesn't necessarily work to women's advantage: they may well lose out because they have less power than men, so that when new opportunities arise, such as education, males monopolise the available resources.

Similarly, **dependency theorists** argue that the decision-making **elites** in Third World societies are based mainly in the **urban metropolis**, so educational resources are diverted away from the countryside. This is part of the systematic **under-development** of the **rural satellite** areas by the city. Also, financial aid for education often does not get through to rural areas due to corruption among officials.

Claire makes a good point about the **lack of relevance of much Third World education** to development goals. You should examine **explanations** of this, such as **Illich's** ideas (e.g. that **cultural imperialism** continues in the post-colonial era, so Third World societies continue to model their education systems on those of their former colonial masters).

You could also follow up Claire's point about irrelevant university education by some reference to different levels and types, e.g. the **need for mass primary education and the benefits of universal literacy**. You could refer to countries (e.g. Cuba, Tanzania) where this has been a major aim of education.

Another area to consider is the **political and ideological** role of education. Critics argue that it is used to build support for authoritarian rulers. **Freire** argues that it could be used to **liberate the masses** by developing a revolutionary consciousness.

Claire needs a brief **conclusion** to pull her answer together. She could draw on one or other of the various **critical perspectives** on development (e.g. dependency theory, Illich) to give some overview. For example, she could explain that inequalities and inadequacies in Third World education exist because of the exploitative nature of Third World societies and of the wider capitalist world system which subordinates them.

Don't forget ...

In 'identify and briefly explain' questions, make sure you develop the explanation part of the answer clearly.

In 'examine' questions, you need to put your points into a sociological context, using concepts, theories and/or evidence from studies.

2 Assess the arguments and evidence for and against the view that foreign aid is an obstacle to the development of Third World countries.

[40 marks]

CLAIRE'S ANSWER

The First World gives the Third World aid for many different reasons, for example due to natural disasters such as earthquakes or floods, or civil wars and conflicts. However, this aid comes at a very high price — namely the interest they have to pay on it. This then gives First World countries a hold over the Third World and allows them to exploit them, and the Third World cannot cope without this aid and so they depend on the First World to give it to them.

Frank's dependency theory is relevant here. Frank argues that the Third World is dependent on the First World. However, the First World uses this to its advantage and exploits the Third World. The First World controls food prices, and deliberately keeps them low to maintain their own high standard of living. The First World deliberately under-develops the Third World, and so it becomes dependent on the First World for things such as aid. Also, a lot of aid money gets spent on things that are not needed or are harmful to the environment, and it gets spent with western companies not local ones, so the West is just recycling it back to itself.

The aid received from the West is short-term help with a long-term benefit but the amount they have to pay back because of the vast interest is a long-term problem. Wallerstein said that core nations such as the UK and the USA exploit the peripheral ones such as India and the countries of Africa.

The development of a country takes place in five steps according to Rostow's theory of modernisation. A country develops in five stages — this however is very vague, and countries don't start from scratch but have often been going for years. Modernisation theorists do not mention aid from other countries as a help to development.

Very brief and unlinked to aid.

'Lack of communication' is only one reason for slow development. Claire's 2nd sentence repeats her point from paragraph 1. The last two sentences contain interesting points but need links to aid. And not all satellites are small (e.g. India)!

Claire's not making much headway here. Much of this is a repeat of paragraphs 1 and 3. The point about Marxism is good but deserves a lot more attention, linking it to Frank or other theorists.

She should link the 'chain of exploitation' to the metropolis-satellite relationship in paragraph 6. But it still needs linking to aid – not just to food prices.

Claire does the right thing in linking her conclusion back to the question of whether aid is an obstacle – but it could do with some opposing views. Good final point about the relative unimportance of aid.

The First World also exploits the Third World through its cheap labour and cheap raw materials, to produce goods for sale in the First World.

The Third World is developing slowly because of lack of communication like faxes and the internet, so aid from the First World should enable the country to develop more quickly. But paying back the aid means the country is once again dependent on the First World. A metropolis is an economic power — like the USA; a satellite is a small, undeveloped country which is dependent on the metropolis. However, there is now some home-grown development within countries — which are termed the Newly Industrialised Countries like Brazil and Mexico.

The First World only helps the Third World in order to benefit themselves. For example, having factories in Third World countries keeps costs low because of cheap labour and raw materials, which is a benefit for the First World. Aid means the Third World has to pay back a lot more money to the First World. The First World exploit the Third to benefit themselves. Just like Marxism, where the bourgeoisie who owned the means of production exploited the workers who worked for them.

The chain of exploitation is the First World exploiting the Third World, the supermarkets in the First World exploit the suppliers in the Third World who in turn exploit the farmers just so the First World can benefit from low food prices.

Although aid does initially help countries to develop a little more, it can mean them actually going backwards rather than forwards in terms of development because they have to repay the First World and so end up back where they started off in the first place — namely, dependent on the First World countries who are exploiting them in every way possible. Aid from the First World is more of an obstacle than a help because it is short-term help but a long-term cost. However, we should also remember that even if foreign aid is an obstacle, the amount provided is actually not very much anyway, and so is not likely to be a major problem. Many other factors, like foreign investors creaming off profits or the low level of education in most Third World countries, are a much bigger obstacle to development than foreign aid.

22/40

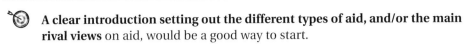

- A clear introduction setting out the different types of aid, and/or the main rival views on aid, would be a good way to start.

- Ensure you have a sound, detailed knowledge of relevant theories. Claire shows knowledge of some potentially relevant material, such as modernisation and dependency theories, but her knowledge is rather limited and sometimes thin. Sharpen up your account of the different theories with key concepts of each theory like cultural diffusion, neo-colonialism, the development of underdevelopment, the Capitalist World System etc.

- Keep focused on the question. Claire has only limited success in linking what she knows about the different theories to the question of aid. Beware of drifting off into a general account of modernisation, dependency etc. without reference to aid. Link your knowledge of theories to the question.

- Similarly, tie in your knowledge of evidence to the question. For example, Claire refers several times to low food prices, but never succeeds in linking this to aid. One way would be to look at how low food prices leave Third World farmers destitute and in need of aid.

- Deal with everything the question asks for: arguments and evidence, for and against the view.

- Arguments could come from different theories – such as modernisation and dependency theories – but other approaches are also relevant. For example, Bauer's market liberal view that aid undermines enterprise and development, or ecological views about the environmental damage caused by large-scale, 'top-down' aid such as dam-building, or ideas of aid as cultural imperialism (e.g. Illich's notion of 'cola colonialism') could all be applied to this question. Ensure you employ the key concepts of the theories you deal with.

- You should draw on evidence from studies of aid such as Hayter's *Aid as Imperialism*, or particular aid projects (e.g. dam-building in India, Turkey etc.).

- You should look at different types of aid (humanitarian/emergency, long term, military, tied aid, food aid etc.), sources of aid (governments, non-governmental organisations like Oxfam, international agencies like the UN or EU, loans from businesses etc.), who controls the aid (e.g. bureaucrats, capitalists, foreign experts, local communities). Try to evaluate the effects of these different types and sources.

- Claire has a conclusion, but yours could be better by ensuring it re-visits a couple of the main arguments for and against aid.

Don't forget ...

Questions on aspects of development always need theories, but you must link them to the specific question – whether on aid, population, education, gender or whatever the question asks.

Modernisation theory and dependency theory are not the only explanations. Make sure you know about others (e.g. ecological, feminist and market liberal views, Warren, Illich or others).

Key points to remember

Definitions of development: There is disagreement about what counts as development and how to measure it. Some see it as economic growth or industrialisation, and measure it in terms of increases in average income. Critics argue that averages conceal inequalities between rich and poor, and that development means more than just economic growth. For example, democracy, literacy, and an unpolluted environment might all be seen as development. Some sociologists take an ecological perspective: development must be sustainable to be 'real' development.

Explanations of development/under-development: Many differences between theories of development and under-development hinge on how they see the relationships between the developed countries and the less developed countries. **Modernisation theory** is functionalist-influenced. It sees the West as having a beneficial effect, and argues that Third World societies must adopt Western values and institutions if they are to develop. **Dependency theory** sees the Western metropolis using its economic, political and military power to exploit and actively under-develop its Third World satellites, perpetuating their subordination. **Marxist modernisation theory** sees this exploitation as having a beneficial effect in transforming Third World countries into capitalist societies, thereby paving the way for socialist revolution. Increased **globalisation** in recent decades has strengthened the inter-connections between different societies and economies, though sociologists disagree as to whether or not this trend spells the end of the Third World's subordination.

Development strategies: Sociologists have different views about the best strategy for achieving development. **Modernisation theorists** favour strengthening the links between the West and Third World society through foreign aid, trade links, foreign investment by trans-national corporations, and the activities of international agencies like the World Bank. **Dependency theorists** see the best chance of development coming from severing, not strengthening, ties with the West. They see aid as a form of imperialism, coming with strings attached, or syphoned off by corrupt officials. **Neo-liberal theorists** see aid hindering development by preventing the free market working efficiently. Food aid has been blamed for increasing the risk of famine by undercutting local farmers and driving them out of business.

Sociologists are interested in different aspects of development: Urbanisation refers to the growth of cities. For the first time in history, there are now more urban- than rural-dwellers. However, urbanisation does not necessarily mean development. Many large Third World cities, though more prosperous than the countryside, often contain largely insecure **employment**, as well as poor housing in shanty-towns. On the other hand, they also contain wealthy economic and political elites, often linked closely to the capitalist world system. **Industrialisation** brings higher incomes and has occurred to varying extents in Third World countries, often linked to world capitalism (e.g. providing cheap labour for mass production of exportable consumer goods). Many Third World countries face severe **environmental problems**, because of the use of out-dated technology, or over-exploitation of resources by foreign capitalism or by the poor in search of a livelihood.

Sociologists are also interested in aspects of development such as education, health, population and gender. Modernisation theorists see **education** as the key means of promoting development by spreading modern Western values and skills, whereas dependency theorists see it as a means of perpetuating the Third World's cultural dependence. Others point to great inequalities in educational provision, between town and country, males and females, rich and poor. **Health** is often used as an indicator of development. Most Third World countries have worse health than the West, but more equal Third World societies tend to have lower death rates. Modernisation theorists often favour Western medical know-how as the solution, but others prefer a social model of health that tackles poverty and inequality. Many writers see **population growth** as the major obstacle to development, but it can also stimulate demand and economic growth. There are also signs that growth rates are beginning to fall, though some argue that Third World countries will not be able to reduce birth rates significantly until there is greater economic security. One measure of development is the extent of **gender** equality (e.g. in literacy rates, voting rights). Sometimes development can create greater opportunities for women (e.g. in employment), but it may also create greater burdens for them (e.g. with the loss of extended family support) and so what may be 'development' for men may not be for women.

Question to try

Part One

Item A

Urbanisation involves a shift in a country's population, from one largely living in the countryside to one largely living in towns and cities. Urban growth simply means the growth of towns and cities. However, although it is not usually possible to have urbanisation without urban growth, it is quite possible to have urban growth without urbanisation. In many Third World societies, even as the cities grow rapidly, so too   5
does the rural population, so that the proportion of city-dwellers to rural-dwellers remains much the same. And even though the towns grow, this does not always bring economic development.

This is very different from the pattern followed in Western societies. For example, in 19th century Britain, despite rapid population growth, there was genuine urbanisation,   10
so that by the end of the century, Britain had been transformed from a largely rural society into a mainly urban one. In the British case, rapid population growth, rapid urbanisation and successful economic development went hand-in-hand. In many Third World countries, by contrast, rapid urban growth and rapid population growth occur without successful urbanisation and without successful economic development.   15

1 (a) Identify and briefly describe **two** reasons why urban growth 'does not always bring economic development' (**Item A, lines 7–8**).

[8 marks]

(b) Using material from **Item A** and elsewhere, examine some of the ways in which population and development may be related.

[12 marks]

Part Two

Answer **one** question from this Part.

2 Assess the usefulness of dependency theory to an understanding of development and under-development.

[40 marks]

3 Assess the nature and extent of the health problems faced by Third World societies and strategies for solving these problems.

[40 marks]

Examiner's hints

● For question **2** you need to be familiar with the key ideas of dependency theory and with the main criticisms made of it by other theories. Beware of simply doing a 'modernisation versus dependency theory' answer that just lists the features of each theory. Instead, try to use your knowledge of modernisation theory to criticise dependency theory. You should also know about other theories (e.g. Warren) and try to apply dependency theory to issues like aid, trade etc.
● For question **3** you need to look at three things: the nature, the extent, and the strategies for solving the Third World's health problems. Put your answer into a theoretical context: different theories will have different views about what the problems and solutions are.

Answers can be found on pages 81–85.

4 Theory and Methods

Exam Question and Answer

Part One

Item A

Questionnaires are probably the most widely used sociological research method. They have a number of attractions to sociologists. For example, many positivist sociologists argue that questionnaires produce reliable, quantifiable data and that this makes them useful in testing hypotheses and establishing correlations and causal relationships. Questionnaires also have several practical advantages over other primary methods: 5 they are a relatively quick, cheap way to study large numbers of people.

Item B

Secondary data are data that already exist. Sociologists make use of a great many different types of data from secondary sources, sometimes employing them to complement primary methods such as questionnaires or interviews. Secondary data include official and other statistics; government reports; documents produced by public bodies, such as birth certificates or school reports; parish records; letters and diaries; even paintings can provide secondary data. Data from such secondary sources 5 as these offer many advantages to the sociologist. Yet there are many problems associated with data from secondary sources and they must be treated with great caution.

1   (a) Identify **one** advantage of using secondary data in sociological research (**Item B, line 7**). [2 marks]

    (b) Suggest **two** ways in which secondary data might be used to complement questionnaires. [4 marks]

    (c) Suggest **three** problems in using letters and/or diaries in sociological research (**Item B lines 5–6**). [6 marks]

    (d) Identify and briefly explain **two** reasons why questionnaires may not produce valid data. [8 marks]

Part Two

Answer **one** question from this Part.

2   Assess the usefulness of observational techniques in sociological research. [40 marks]

3   'Sociology is often seen as divided into two distinct approaches: ones based on the concept of social structure or social system, and ones based on the concept of social action.' Assess the value of social action approaches to an understanding of society. [40 marks]

ELISA'S ANSWER

1 (a) Identify **one** advantage of using secondary data in sociological research (**Item B, line 7**).

[2 marks]

One advantage of using secondary sources of data in research is clearly that it can save time if someone else has already collected the data that you need. For instance, if you wanted to study inequality in health, it would be much quicker to draw on data already collected by the NHS or government for the whole country instead of having to try and obtain it through your own research.

(2/2)

1 (b) Suggest **two** ways in which secondary data might be used to complement questionnaires.

[4 marks]

One way is to suggest questions to use in the questionnaire. For example, if you studied national statistics on the subject you were interested in, it might reveal patterns — e.g. that young males commit more crime than females. This might then suggest the idea that you could ask questions to try to discover why this pattern was occurring.

Another way is to test out your findings from your other research. For example, if you had done participant observation (PO) with one small group, you could complement this with a postal questionnaire to a much larger group, with the insights you had gained from the PO being used to suggest questions to ask in the questionnaire.

(2/4)

1 (c) Suggest **three** problems in using letters and/or diaries in sociological research (**Item B, lines 5–6**).

[6 marks]

One problem in using letters or diaries in sociological research is that they are written documents. If you are studying a group that is illiterate, or a culture that doesn't have writing, they won't have produced any written documents.

Some people lie or exaggerate when writing things down. For example, a famous general or politician may play down his failures in his diaries (e.g. blaming others for a defeat in battle), knowing that others will probably read them when he is dead.

They might be forgeries — e.g. the famous case of 'Hitler's diaries' in the 1990s. It was claimed that someone had discovered Hitler's war diaries. If true, this would have been very valuable to historians and social scientists, but unfortunately they were forgeries.

(6/6)

1 (d) Identify and briefly explain **two** reasons why questionnaires may not produce valid data.

[8 marks]

One reason why questionnaires may not always produce valid data is because they often have a low response rate. For example, many questionnaires (especially postal ones) have extremely low response rates because people can't be bothered to fill them out, go and post them etc. Sometimes they may even have been filled out by a different person from the one that the researcher wanted to complete the form.

Another reason why questionnaires don't produce valid data is because people may not understand the question properly, so in a way they are answering a different question from the one they have been asked, but unfortunately the researcher doesn't necessarily know this, so he/she is unwittingly getting a false picture of people's views.

6/8

How to score full marks

 For part **1 (a)**, full marks here – but Elisa need not have written any more after the first sentence (although her example is a good one and shows a clear understanding).

In **1 (b)**, the first point is fine and scores two marks, but the second one does not score for two reasons: it's really a **repeat** of the previous point about suggesting questions, and in any case PO is a **primary rather a secondary source**. A better point would be to say you could use a **qualitative** secondary source (e.g. letters) to complement the **quantitative** primary data from the questionnaire, **thus gaining both valid and reliable data**.

Full marks for **1 (c)** – all three are problems of using letters and diaries. Others include the **problem of interpreting their meaning** (e.g. if written in archaic, foreign or technical language), or the fact that even in literate societies not everyone keeps a diary or writes letters so they may be **unrepresentative**.

In answer to question **1 (d)** you need to be clear that **validity means getting a true or authentic picture of the thing you are studying**. Elisa's first paragraph actually identifies two different reasons – a **low response rate**, and being **filled out by the wrong person**. Her second paragraph identifies a third reason – respondents **not understanding the question**. All of these are correct – they would all prevent us getting a true picture – but Elisa only explains the last one properly. To explain low response rate, you could say that **those who do respond might be very different from those who don't – so giving a distorted picture of how the sample as a whole thinks or acts.**

Don't forget ...

When asked for a certain number of points, you won't be penalised for giving more if you want. But make sure that you **explain them properly** when asked to do so.

Reliability, validity and representativeness are key concepts. Make sure you can define them clearly and apply them to different methods and sources of data.

2 Assess the usefulness of observational techniques in sociological research.

[40 marks]

ELISA'S ANSWER

Observational techniques are widely used in sociology, especially by interactionists and other interpretive approaches. Interactionists favour the use of participant observation because it enables them to get close to the group they are studying. By joining in or participating in the group's way of life, the sociologist can get a first-hand feeling for what it is like to be a member of that group and so gain insight into their meanings and what makes them 'tick'.

A good example of this is Eileen Barker's study of the Unification Church, better known as the Moonies. She used overt participant observation, where the group knew that they were being studied by a sociologist. She found that contrary to media and popular views, members were not brainwashed but joined of their own free will, and that most of them came from normal, secure backgrounds. Using overt observation meant that she could be honest with the Moonies and didn't have to deliberately lie or conceal anything to gain entry to the group.

However, it is not always possible to be overt when joining a group that you wish to study. For example, some groups would probably not want to be studied, so if the researcher was completely open about themselves they would not be able to gain access and the study would be over before it had begun. This is likely to be true if the group has something to hide, such as a deviant or criminal group. For example, Humphreys used covert participant observation in his study 'Tea Room Trade' — a study of male homosexual activity in public toilets. In this he pretended to be one of the group, taking the role of 'watch queen' or look-out. This enabled him to observe as if he were a member of the group while at the same time not participating in the sexual activity himself. He argues that if you want to study a deviant group, you have to pretend to be in the same boat as they are or otherwise they will not trust you enough to let you into the group.

On the other hand, Polsky has criticised this approach. He argues that you should be open, i.e. use overt PO. His reason is that if you claim to be one of the group, they will eventually put you to the test and if they find out your true identity, this could have serious consequences, especially if it is a criminal group. There are

---

A useful start, linking methods to perspectives – but note that observational techniques include non-participant observation as well as PO.

A definition and relevant example of overt PO.

Good arguments and evidence for covert methods – though it would be a good idea to use the term.

Good counter-arguments against covert methods – but no mention of ethical issues.

other criticisms that can be made of covert PO. One is that it can be very difficult to carry it off — you need to have a carefully constructed cover story, and have to know a lot about the group already so you know how to act and speak etc. when you join it. This might be hard to do, especially if they are a secretive or deviant group, and if they aren't, you could probably use overt PO anyway.

Once you are accepted into the group, there are problems staying in and problems getting out. Some sociologists become over-attached to the group and start to over-identify with it. Gradually they become absorbed into the group — as Whyte said, 'I started off as a non-participating observer and ended up as a non-observing participant.' When it comes to getting out, it might be more difficult if you have been a covert observer, because you will need a convincing 'story' — unless you just abandon them.

The main advantage of participant observation is that it gives a great deal of insight into a group. This means it is particularly useful for studying deviant or 'outsider' groups that sociologists would not normally spend their time in. It is also much favoured by interactionists because they seek to gain access to people's meanings and experiences, and by joining in they can develop a personal understanding of these things. This enables them to achieve validity, which is their main aim in sociological research.

However, positivists such as functionalists and Marxists dislike methods such as participant observation because they don't give a wider view of society. They are very unscientific and too small scale for positivists to make use of in their research.

26/40

How to score full marks

- **Read the question carefully!** This one asks about 'observational techniques'. Elisa covers two types of participant observation, but you should also make at least a brief reference to **non-participant** observation. You could link this to more **positivist** approaches, to contrast with the link between PO and interpretive perspectives.

- **Beware of drifting into describing the findings** of the studies – **focus instead on the methods** they used. Elisa's account of Barker comes close to this. If you describe the findings, you need to show how the method used did (or didn't) enable the researcher to gain these results (e.g. Barker was able to contradict media/commonsense views of the Moonies and get at the truth about them).

- Elisa gives a good account of several **practical issues** involved in PO (e.g. getting out, problems of covert observation, going native), though you could mention some others – such as the **observer's presence** affecting the group's behaviour, the **time** taken to carry out PO, or the problem of accurately **recording/remembering** events and comments.

- You also need **more discussion of theoretical issues** than Elisa. She mentions some **positivist counter-arguments** at the end, but you should develop these further. These include over-involvement leading to a biased view and **loss of proper scientific detachment and objectivity**. Structuralists also argue that a full understanding of a group cannot be obtained simply by studying their meanings (e.g. through PO), since **structural forces of which the group may be unaware** still shape their lives, and PO tells us little about these.

- Many of these **theoretical problems can be linked to methodological ones**. For example, the observer's lack of objectivity means that observations may simply be reflections of the observer's own personal selective perceptions, so PO findings may not even be valid – they merely give the observer's view of reality, rather than the reality itself.

- Similarly, the small scale of PO means **lack of representativeness**, making **generalisation and theorisation difficult**. The very personal nature of PO means that it cannot easily be repeated, making it an **unreliable** source of data.

- **Ethical issues** are worth mentioning – especially in relation to **covert** methods. Should we be deceiving and spying on those we study? Should we break the law in the course of participating?

- Elisa mentions several **studies** – but there are many more you could use, such as Patrick, Ditton, Festinger, Pryce, etc.

Don't forget ...

It's always worth looking at any given method in terms of both its **practical** and its **theoretical** aspects – and **ethical** aspects, where applicable.

'**Observation**' includes non-participant techniques. If the question does not specify PO, you should say something about these, too (although you would not be expected to make it a major part of your answer).

Key points to remember

'Theory and Methods' at A2 level overlaps with material in the AQA Unit 3, 'Sociological Methods'. This is outlined in *Do Brilliantly AS Sociology*. For A2, you need to be familiar with this – and with the material below.

Sociological theories: Functionalism sees society as based on **consensus** – shared values. Marxists argue that society is characterised by class **conflict**. Other conflict theorists (e.g. Weberians, feminists) argue that conflict and inequality may be based on non-class factors, such as power or status, or on gender. Theories can also be divided into **structural and action**. The former (e.g. functionalism, Marxism) see society as a structure 'out there' that turns individuals into puppets whose role is to meet the system's needs. The latter (e.g. interactionism) see individuals as having free will and determining their own actions through the meanings they give to situations.

Sociology and science: Positivists argue that sociology can and should be scientific. They take the natural sciences as their model, including **quantitative methods** and the search for **causal laws**. **Interpretivists** reject this, arguing that humans are not like rocks or atoms. Because we have consciousness and free will, our behaviour is not 'caused' like that of atoms, so different kinds of explanation and **qualitative methods** are needed, to achieve an **understanding** of actors' meanings. To complicate matters further, there are disagreements about what 'science' is anyway. **Popper** argues that it involves falsification of theories, not verification as positivists believe. **Kuhn** argues that sociology does not have a paradigm (a shared view of what the subject is about) and is thus not yet a science.

The relationship between theory and methods: Positivists prefer quantitative sources and methods, such as official statistics or questionnaires, since these allow us to identify correlations, to test hypotheses, and to establish causal laws. **Interpretivists** prefer qualitative methods and sources – such as PO, diaries and letters – since these allow us to get close to the subject's reality and achieve verstehen (empathetic understanding) rather than causal explanations. However, the relationship between theories and methods is not clear-cut – e.g. functionalist anthropologists (associated with positivism) have used PO to study other cultures.

Subjectivity, objectivity, and value freedom: Sociologists are part of what they study (i.e. society), so is it possible to be detached and objective – or must their own personal values or subjectivity affect what and how they study and what they find? If the latter, is their knowledge worth anything, since it only reflects their own values, not 'reality'? **Positivists** argue that sociologists can and should be objective, while **interpretivists** argue that we cannot understand social reality without being involved in it and, therefore, we should take the side of the underdog. **Marxists** argue that sociological knowledge serves class interests. **Weber** argued that it is possible to be value-free, but the choice of topic and the use to which the findings are put will be affected by the sociologist's values. Others argue that those who **fund** the research impose their values on it.

Sociology and social policy: Sociology seeks to answer theoretical questions about society; social policy seeks to solve practical problems. **Early positivists**, and **Marx**, believed we could gain a scientific understanding of the laws governing social development and so plan a more rational society. **Popper** believed that the role of sociology was 'piecemeal social engineering' – designing changes to specific institutions to improve their functioning. **Wright Mills** argues that although this gives sociologists 'expert' status, it turns them into servants of the state and big business.

Modernity/modernism and postmodernity/postmodernism: Modernity is a period characterised economically by capitalism, politically by the democratic nation state, and culturally by reason not tradition. It came into existence through the scientific, political and industrial revolutions of the 17th–19th centuries. **Modernism** believes that rational understanding and control of the world is possible. Sociology is part of the modernist project – an attempt to use scientific principles to achieve true, general explanations of society to enable us to control its development. Some writers believe we now live in an age of **postmodernity** characterised by uncertainty. The pace of change quickens, the spread of a global culture and economy break down boundaries of time and space, and social relationships become fluid. **Postmodernism** believes that this fragmentation and rapid change mean that it is not now possible to have rational knowledge of society – a view most sociologists reject. Giddens argues that we are in an era of **late modernity**.

Part One

Item A

Laboratory experiments offer researchers the advantage of being able to test the effect of different variables upon their subjects in a controlled environment. They are also said to be one of the best ways of gaining reliable data.

However, laboratory experiments are not widely used in sociology. For one thing, the use of such experiments can pose a number of ethical problems for the researcher. 5 Even if these can be overcome, there are serious doubts as to whether laboratory experiments can ever produce valid data.

Item B

Unstructured interviews are frequently used to examine closely people's feelings or attitudes. Unlike in a structured interview, the interviewer in an unstructured interview does not have a fixed set of precisely worded questions drawn up in advance, but rather just a mental checklist of issues. The interviewer's job is to try to steer the interview so that these issues can be covered, and this makes the interview more like a 'guided 5 conversation'. Of course, this has its drawbacks: for example, the interviewer may not remember to cover all the issues. Despite this, however, many sociologists prefer to use unstructured rather than structured interviews.

1 (a) Describe **one** advantage, apart from the one referred to in **Item B**, in not having a 'fixed set of precisely worded questions' (**Item B, line 3**).

[2 marks]

(b) Explain the difference between reliable data (**Item A, line 3**) and valid data (**Item A, line 7**).

[4 marks]

(c) Suggest **three** reasons why some sociologists prefer to use unstructured rather than structured interviews (**Item B**).

[6 marks]

(d) Identify and briefly describe **two** ethical problems faced by researchers using laboratory experiments (**Item A, line 5**).

[8 marks]

Part Two

Answer **one** question from this Part.

2 Assess the extent to which it is possible to describe sociology as a scientific discipline.

[40 marks]

3 Assess the value of Marxist approaches to the study of society.

[40 marks]

Examiner's hints

● For question **2**, look at positivist and interpretivist views of whether sociology can be scientific, including issues such as causal laws, experiments, quantitative versus qualitative data, consciousness, meaning and verstehen. It is also relevant to look at what we mean by '(natural) science' (e.g. Popper, Kuhn) to decide if it is a suitable model for sociology.

● For **3**, you should look at both 'classical' and 'neo'-Marxism, and at issues and concepts like the base/superstructure model, materialism, determinism, ideology, and the primacy of class. Consider the views of Gramsci, Althusser, Gouldner or other Marxists. Views from other perspectives (functionalism, Weber, interactionism, feminism, postmodernism) could be used in evaluation.

Answers can be found on pages 86–90.

Synoptic assessment

Synoptic assessment is an important part of all A2 exams. Synoptic assessment tests your knowledge and understanding of the subject as a whole, including how the different aspects that you have studied are related. For this reason, the exam paper containing the synoptic assessment can only be taken at the end of your course.

For AQA's A2 Sociology, **Unit 6 is the synoptic unit**. This offers you a choice of topics: either **Crime and Deviance**, or **Stratification and Differentiation** (see chapter 6). Whichever of these two topics you choose, the questions will test your knowledge and understanding of the links between that topic and three other things:

- other topics you have studied at AS and/or A2
- sociological theories
- sociological methods.

Links between Crime and Deviance and other AS/A2 topics

You won't have studied all the topics in the specification. This does not matter, because the questions are set so that you will be neither advantaged nor disadvantaged by studying some topics rather than others. If you have chosen Crime and Deviance as your synoptic topic, however, you will need to be able to show that you understand how it links to the other topics that you have studied in the other AS and A2 units.

There is not space here to list every single link between Crime and Deviance and the other ten topics in the specification. Instead, what I have done is to give you examples of some of these links. Thinking about these connections between topics – and trying to think of other ones for the topics you have studied – is a good way to prepare for your exam.

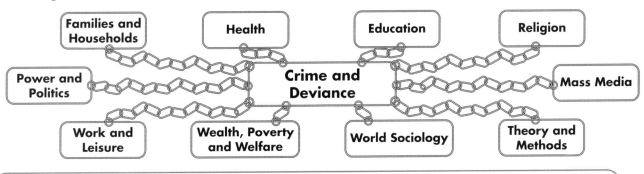

 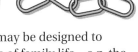

Families and Households

- A key function of the family is **primary socialisation** – which involves learning to **conform** to society's expectations. Marxists see this conformity as a form of **social control** to benefit capitalism, producing workers who do not **rebel**. Feminists see the family instilling conformity to gender role norms.

- Some writers, notably the **New Right**, see **changing patterns** and **increasing diversity** of family life – such as the increase in lone parent and gay households, cohabitation and births outside marriage – as **deviant**. They see lone parents as failing to socialise children adequately, producing **juvenile delinquency**. Some sociologists see the family as socialising individuals into **deviant subcultures**.

- Laws and **state policies** may be designed to encourage certain **norms** of family life – e.g. the Child Support Agency may aim to encourage fathers to take financial responsibility for their families; making rape within marriage a crime may promote greater equality between spouses.

- Changing norms and **expectations about family roles** – e.g. those of women – mean that what was once considered deviant may now be normal (e.g. women working). Historical and cross-cultural differences in **the position of children** show how what is seen as 'normal' for children is **socially constructed**.

- **Feminists** note how **domestic violence** against women is often regarded as trivial by police and courts. Also, because it takes place in the private sphere, its true extent may be hidden.

Health

- The **medical model** of health and illness sees health as the norm and **sickness and disability as deviation**. Functionalists such as Parsons see **the sick role** as a means of controlling this deviance.

- Most sociologists see the **medical profession** as having a **social control** function. For example, Marxists see doctors as enforcing work discipline for the benefit of capitalism by controlling access to sick leave, while feminists see medicine as reinforcing women's conformity to patriarchal norms.

- Some sociologists explain social **inequalities in health** (such as the higher morbidity and mortality rates among the lower classes, males and some ethnic minorities) as the result of **deviant** or inappropriate **subcultural values** that lead them into health-damaging behaviour. For example, working-class males may value short-term hedonism and 'macho' behaviour such as heavy drinking, or have a fatalistic attitude to their health.

- **Mental illness** is widely regarded as a form of **deviance**. **Interactionists** such as Lemert see it as the outcome of interaction, negotiation and **negative labelling** by professionals and others. Cross-cultural **differences in behavioural norms**, together with **stereotyping** by ethnocentric professionals, may lead to more **black people** being labelled as mentally ill.

Mass Media

- The mass media are a key source of **definitions of reality and normality** in today's society. Functionalists see the media as **reflecting a value consensus**, while Marxists see the media as **engineering** a consensus in the interests of the ruling class.

- The media play a central role in the **social construction of crime and deviance** (e.g. in creating and spreading ideas about what crimes are prevalent, what criminals are like etc.) and in shaping **societal reactions** to deviance. For example, Cohen and Hall *et al* both show the media's role in **amplifying deviance** and creating **moral panics** (e.g. identifying **scapegoats** such as mods and rockers, or black youth) and mobilising the public, politicians and **agents of social control** to deal with them. Young shows how the media help to shape police and public perceptions of **drug users**.

- Marxists argue that the media serve the interests of capitalism by being able to portray those who oppose or threaten it – such as strikers or protesters – as **mindless or irrational**. The mass media may represent other groups, such as gays or the disabled, as **abnormal**. Feminists see the media as acting as a form of **social control** over women by defining acceptable roles and behaviour for them.

- The hypodermic syringe model sees the mass media as having the **power to influence** their audiences to commit **deviant or criminal acts**, such as 'copycat crimes'.

Education

- Subcultural theorists explain **underachievement** of working-class pupils in terms of **socialisation into class subcultures** that do not value education or provide the skills and attitudes needed for educational success. By comparison with mainstream culture, these subcultures are **deviant**.

- By contrast, interactionists explain unequal attainment as the result of the **labelling** process, in which some pupils are judged **deviant** – i.e. seen as not conforming to the school's rules or ethos. Pupils from working class and some ethnic minority backgrounds are likely to be defined by teachers in terms of **negative stereotypes**, which they may internalise and then, through the **self-fulfilling prophecy**, act out their deviant label, often together with others similarly labelled, in **anti-school pupil subcultures**.

- From a functionalist perspective, education is a key **agency of secondary socialisation** and can be seen as helping to **secure conformity** to society's rules and commitment to its goals by integrating individuals into a shared culture.

 # Wealth, Poverty and Welfare

- To be in **poverty can be seen as a form of deviance** – it is regarded as an undesirable, **stigmatised status** by the majority of society and those occupying this status may be perceived as inferior, unacceptable or 'outsiders'. Some perspectives, such as the **New Right**, reflect this – e.g. Murray sees the **underclass** as a **deviant 'new rabble'**, in which males are prone to **criminality**, while **deviant female-headed, lone-parent families** are widespread.
- Lewis' **culture of poverty thesis** suggests that the poor are simultaneously both **conformists** (conforming to their own subcultural values) and **deviants** (deviating from the culture of wider society).
- **Functionalists** see the poor as those who have **failed to conform** by not achieving in terms of society's meritocratic value system. From a **Marxist** perspective, private capitalist **wealth** is in effect **'criminal'** or immoral, since it is acquired through the exploitation of the labour of others.
- The **New Right** sees **social policy** – especially an over-generous welfare state – as the main **cause of the deviant underclass**. Policy should have **moral** objectives – namely to secure **conformity to respectable values** such as the conventional family and self-reliance. **Marxists** see the welfare state as a form of **social control** over the proletariat (e.g. coercing the unemployed into accepting low-paid jobs), while **feminists** see it as a form of social control over women.

 # Work and Leisure

- **Work** provides opportunities to commit **crime**, ranging from pilfering by factory workers to **white-collar crime** by those in positions of status and power. Marxists argue that **crimes of the powerful** – committed by capitalists and other elite groups – are less likely to be detected, prosecuted or punished.
- Workers are expected to obey **workplace norms** – such as punctuality and productivity – and are supervised and punished by **formal sanctions**, such as dismissal, for failing to conform to these. **Informal work groups** may establish their own norms, however – as Mayo discovered – and exercise **social control** over members' behaviour through **informal sanctions**.
- **Functionalists** see **industrial conflict as deviant**, whereas **Marxists** see it as the **norm** in capitalist society. Some forms of conflict may be regarded as more deviant than others (e.g. those involving violence or sabotage).
- **Technological innovations** may increase the potential for **surveillance and control** of the workforce by employers.
- In a society where **paid work is the expected norm** and a major source of identity, the **unemployed** may be seen as **deviant** (e.g. as 'scroungers') and unemployment may be a **cause of criminality**. Large-scale unemployment may become a **threat to social order**.
- Some sociologists see **delinquency as a 'solution'** to the problem of adolescent working-class **leisure**. The powerful may control working-class leisure to maintain **social order**.

 # Power and Politics

- **Functionalists** argue that power benefits everyone in society. There is a **consensus** on who should exercise it, and this maintains **social order**. **Marxists** argue that power enables the ruling class to maintain **social control** through their control of **the state**. This also enables them to make the criminal **law** in their interests to protect their property and privileges.
- The notion of **deviant voters** has been used in the past to describe those who vote against the party seen as representing their class interests – i.e. working-class Conservative and middle-class Labour voters.
- Other forms of political participation have been seen as **deviant** in another sense. Some **political movements** may be seen as deviant in terms

Power and Politics (continued)

of either the goals that they pursue (such as achieving a one-party state), or the means they use to achieve these goals (e.g. terrorism), or both. Other movements may use illegal but non-violent forms of direct action, such as obstructing access to land (e.g. protests against road-builders).

- The **media** play a major part in the political process, and they may be used to portray a political party's policies or leaders as **deviant** (e.g. suggesting that a party's programme is unpatriotic).

Religion

- Religion is seen by **functionalists** as maintaining **social order** by **integrating** individuals into the value consensus through shared beliefs and rituals; whereas, for **Marxists**, religion maintains **social control** by promoting **false consciousness** among the oppressed so as to secure their continued acceptance of exploitation.

- Religion is often a conservative force, but can be a **source of change**, introducing **new values** that can be seen as deviant from the viewpoint of the old social order. Religious **prophets** have often been **persecuted** for this.

- Many **religious movements and organisations** have been regarded as **deviant**, and some may also break the **criminal** law. Troeltsch distinguished between church and sect, seeing **churches as conforming** to wider cultural norms and integrating individuals into society, whereas **sects** are radical organisations that see society as corrupt. **World-rejecting sects** in particular are often seen as **deviant** by mainstream society. Some religious movements are seen as promoting deviant lifestyles or sexual values (e.g. Mormon polygamy), or as disrupting social order by brainwashing and luring people away from normal family life, career etc.

World Sociology

- **Durkheimian** theories of evolutionary social change stress the importance of a new basis for **social order and integration**, based on the division of labour and the value of individualism.

- **Modernisation theorists** argue that Third World cultures are backward and deviant in terms of the **values and personality-types needed for development**. On this view, successful development requires **new norms** of conduct. For example, modernisation theorists take the view that traditional cultural values concerning the subordinate role of women must be abandoned in favour of 'modern', 'western' values of gender equality. Similarly, **traditional health beliefs and practices** may come to be seen as **deviant and superstitious**.

- **Globalisation theory** suggests that a **single global culture** is coming into being, and thus a **single set of norms** and a global consensus on what is considered unacceptable (e.g. child labour).

- **Ties between First and Third World** can be seen as forms of **control** by the former over the latter. Theresa Hayter sees **aid** as a form of social, political, cultural and economic control over the Third World. Other **dependency theorists**, such as A.G. Frank, make similar arguments about the role of **trade** and about the part played by **international agencies** such as the World Bank and IMF.

- The study of crime and deviance raises many **practical, theoretical and ethical issues** for sociologists. **Practical problems** include the difficulty of gaining access to groups whose behaviour is regarded as disreputable or criminal. For example, it might not be easy to become a **participant observer** in a deviant gang (especially if the observation is covert), while criminals may be suspicious of anyone **trying to conduct a survey**.

- **Theoretical problems** include the dangers of relying on **quantitative** sources such as **official statistics** as valid accounts of crime and deviance, while smaller-scale **qualitative** sources and methods (such as letters and diaries, unstructured interviews or participant observation) may be more valid but fail to give a reliable or representative picture.

- **Ethical issues** include the rights and wrongs of using **covert observational methods** to study deviants or criminals. Is it moral to 'spy' on someone without their knowledge and consent, while pretending to be 'one of them'? Or does a valid knowledge of deviance justify the methods used to obtain it?

- The study of **suicide** raises many of these issues about methods. **Positivists** prefer **quantitative** sources such as **official suicide statistics**, which they see as a useful **resource** for discovering social laws. **Interpretivists** see statistics as a **topic** for investigation to discover how they came to be **socially constructed**, and prefer **qualitative** methods (e.g. the analysis of suicide notes or observation of coroners' courts).

- The debate about suicide also raises issues about whether sociology can be seen as a science. The **positivist Durkheim** used the study of suicide to attempt to show that sociology can be a science, observing social **patterns** such as the suicide rate to identify **social facts** and discovering **laws of cause and effect** to explain them. **Interpretivists** such as Douglas or Atkinson argue instead that the study of suicide demonstrates that sociology must be the study of **human meanings** (e.g. those of the deceased) and of how people **make sense** of the world.

- Deviance raises issues about **objectivity**. **Interactionists** such as Becker argue that sociologists must be committed, not neutral or value free. They should **side with the underdog** – frequently someone whom those with power have labelled a **deviant**. **Functionalists** regard the sociologist as on the side of 'society' **against** deviance, though they also recognise that increased deviance often **indicates a social problem** that needs to be remedied by changes in **policy**. **Positivist** theories of crime often aim to discover the **causes** so as to find **solutions** to the 'problem of crime' (e.g. in the form of strategies for crime reduction).

- **Postmodernist** approaches argue that deviance is a **modernist** concept and depends on the existence of a shared or dominant value system that can define deviance unambiguously. In a **post-modern societ**y, however, it is not possible to identify a single value system and so a single yardstick for what is normal and what is deviant. Therefore, the concept is **no longer meaningful**.

Answer **both** parts of the question.

Part One

Item A

Durkheim held the view that the suicide rate found in any given society was a 'social fact'. For Durkheim, a social fact is greater than the individual; it exists independently of individuals and it exerts an influence over their lives – and, in the case of the suicide rate, an influence over their deaths. Social facts are also fairly constant, and change only gradually. By contrast, while the suicide rate remains constant within a society, it varies   5
between societies, and between groups within a society. Thus Denmark has a higher suicide rate than Ireland, and within a country, the rate is higher for Protestants, urban dwellers and the single, widowed or divorced than it is for Catholics, rural dwellers and married people. For Durkheim, social facts could be measured, quantified and compared. A useful source of social facts are the official statistics published by governments on   10
issues such as crime and suicide.

(a) Identify and briefly explain **two** advantages of using official statistics in the study of crime and deviance (**Item A**).   [8 marks]
[This part of the question tests your knowledge and understanding of the connections between Crime and Deviance and sociological methods.]

(b) Using material from **Item A** and elsewhere, briefly examine some of the problems in explaining suicide rates in terms of social facts.   [12 marks]
[This part of the question tests your knowledge and understanding of the connections between Crime and Deviance and sociological theory.]

Part Two

(c) 'Working-class crime is best understood as a product of the social background of the offender.' Assess this view.   [40 marks]
[This part of the question tests your knowledge and understanding of the connections between Crime and Deviance and other topic(s) that you have studied.]

(a) Identify and briefly explain **two** advantages of using official statistics in the study of crime and deviance (**Item A**).

[8 marks]

KIERAN'S ANSWER

One advantage of using official statistics in studying crime and deviance is that they are already collected for you. The government (Home Office) regularly gather information from courts, police etc. and compile detailed information on the numbers of different crimes reported to the police, the number of convictions, the age and sex of the offenders, and things like verdicts from coroners' courts. However, they don't gather statistics on things like the class background of offenders, which is a pity as this would be very useful to sociologists, since they are often interested in the effect of class position on people's likelihood of committing crime. This information is then published and sociologists, criminologists or others can avail themselves of these facts. Obviously this saves sociologists a lot of time. The other advantage of official statistics often pointed out is that they cover the whole country, because the Home Office publishes national (and sometimes local and regional) statistics.

6/8

> Quite a good answer – the first advantage (statistics are already collected) is identified and well explained – but the second advantage (statistics cover the whole country) isn't really explained.

How to score full marks

- This part of the question is testing your understanding of the **synoptic links** between sociological **methods** and crime and deviance. You need to be aware of how 'methods' issues – in this case, statistics – relate to the study of crime and deviance.

- Make sure you **explain** points when asked to do so. Kieran's second advantage needs a proper explanation – e.g. you could say that the fact that official statistics cover the whole country means that **we can make generalisations from them**.

- **Organise your answer** to questions that ask for two (or three, or four) reasons, points, examples, criticisms etc. **Set each one out on a new line** – maybe then you will remember to explain each one properly, unlike Kieran.

- **Avoid the temptation to include irrelevant material.** Kieran's third sentence ('However, they don't gather statistics on things like the class …') shows he knows something, but it's not something that helps to answer the question.

(b) Using material from **Item A** and elsewhere, briefly examine some of the problems in explaining suicide rates in terms of social facts.

[12 marks]

KIERAN'S ANSWER

Durkheim's approach is based on social facts, as described in Item A. This is quite useful because social facts cover the whole of society, so it enables the researcher to see very easily what the trends are, e.g. is suicide going up or going down or staying at the same rate? If so, why? So it could lead the sociologist to find hypotheses to explain the trends.

> A great way to start a question about the advantages – but this one is about the *problems!*

However, one problem with explanations based on social facts is that Durkheim takes for granted that they really exist. Other sociologists such as Douglas and Atkinson would argue that there is no such thing as social facts, so you cannot use them to explain suicide rates (or anything else). Durkheim makes the mistake of thinking that the suicide rate is accurate. But in fact, it is far from accurate because many deaths are wrongly classified. For example, if an old lady with a painful chronic illness and living alone is found dead in a gas-filled room or with an empty bottle of sleeping tablets next to her, it is automatically assumed by everybody that her death was a suicide, e.g. because she was isolated or suffering. However, we have no way of knowing for sure, so to classify her death as suicide may be inaccurate. Every death wrongly classified makes the suicide rate statistics less reliable.

> Starts with a good point about social facts but does not develop it. It would be useful to deal with Douglas and Atkinson separately. The point about inaccuracy of statistics is relevant but a bit long.

An alternative way to approach suicide is to try to understand the meanings it involves. Douglas uses methods like interviews with survivors, relatives etc., and analysis of suicide notes to try to find out what the death meant to the person who commits (or tries to commit) suicide. From this, Douglas puts suicides into different categories according to their meaning – e.g. as revenge, to gain sympathy, to get to heaven etc. This might be better than Durkheim's idea of classifying suicides into his own categories according to what type of social fact they are (i.e. egoistic, anomic, altruistic or fatalistic), regardless of the meaning they had for the deceased.

> Some quite good material here, but Kieran could make more of what is wrong with Durkheim's approach.

A final problem with using the idea of social facts to explain suicide rates is pointed out by Atkinson. This is that all the deaths in the statistics are actually the result of coroners' decisions so, depending on the interpretations they make, the rate will be high or low. Atkinson (an ethnomethodologist) says this means they are social constructs.

> Good – but more contrast between social facts and social constructs would help.

(6/12)

50

How to score full marks

- This part of the question is testing your understanding of the **synoptic links** between crime and deviance and **sociological theory**. The reference to 'social facts' is the clue here – **positivists see statistical rates** (such as those for suicide or crime) **as social facts**, whereas **interpretivists** see them as merely **social constructs**.

- Kieran starts with a paragraph on advantages. **If the question only asks for the problems, don't waste time on the advantages** (and vice versa) – unless you can find a clear way to link them to the problems!

- **Make more use of the Item** than Kieran does. You could take up points like **differences within and between societies** and use these to raise problems – e.g. that Protestant/Catholic differences may be due to concealment of suicides rather than a lower number of suicides occurring.

- Kieran recognises some of the shortcomings of Durkheim's approach, but tends to **describe** alternative views rather than use them more directly to **raise problems** with the idea of social facts. You could use the previous example about religion to illustrate the point that the rate is **constructed** by the actions of the living (e.g. police destroying suicide notes to 'protect' the relatives).

- Kieran mentions **ethnomethodology**. Explain what this means (the study of the rules that members of society use to make sense of the world – or in this case, the commonsense rules that coroners use to make sense of deaths). Their **verdicts are just interpretations – not facts**. Use this to criticise Durkheim's position – e.g. coroners' rules (and the laws) for arriving at a suicide verdict in Denmark may be different from those used in Ireland – so accounting for different rates.

- You could **link Douglas to interactionism** and **contrast the idea of social facts with the idea of social meanings**.

- A key point to get across is that Durkheim's critics don't see suicide rates as facts – i.e. **they're not 'things out there' existing independently of individuals, but are constructed through human actions and interpretations**.

Don't forget ...

Keep your examples **concise** and **focused**. Don't make them long-winded – there isn't time. Also, ensure that you draw the **sociological point** out of them.

Don't just describe different views – use what you know about one study or theory to highlight and **discuss problems** with other studies/theories.

(c) 'Working-class crime is best understood as a product of the social background of the offender.' Assess this view.

[40 marks]

KIERAN'S ANSWER

Statistics show that some groups in society are more likely to commit crime than others. For example, young, working-class males and especially black males, in inner city areas, are the groups most likely to commit crime. Sociologists have a number of theories as to why this is the case.

A reasonable start – but better to say 'some groups are more likely to be *convicted* of a crime' than 'more likely to *commit* crime'.

Many sociological theories of working-class crime see it as the result of aspects of the offender's class background. Merton, a functionalist, put forward his anomie theory of crime and deviance to link it to class. He came up with five categories — conformity, innovation, ritualism, retreatism and rebellion. All of them were about the relationship between goals and means. In modern society (Merton was writing about America), people are encouraged to aspire to achieve as far as possible and are told that everyone has a fair chance, i.e. it's a meritocracy. They are encouraged to aspire to individual success and material wealth. But unfortunately, not everyone can get the rewards on offer. Even in a meritocracy there are winners and losers, but Merton also recognises that in modern America, some people have a better chance of success because of their backgrounds. Merton looks at how people deal with not being able to achieve society's goals in acceptable ways. Working-class people are less likely to achieve success through education and a normal career, so they are more likely to 'innovate' — i.e. create new means of achieving material success through economic crimes such as theft.

Relevant material used here, linked to issue of 'background'. A good account of Merton's ideas.

However, Merton's theory doesn't explain all working-class crime. For example, although it explains things like theft, it doesn't explain why some working-class people (especially young men) commit crimes where there is no economic gain, e.g. vandalism, brawling, being drunk and disorderly, etc. These are known as non-utilitarian crimes, i.e. there is no material benefit in committing them. Albert Cohen says that many of these crimes can be explained by the idea of subcultures.

Useful evaluation of Merton, and Kieran introduces another approach.

A subculture is a group who have norms and values that are different from the mainstream ones shared by the majority. It arises to compensate people who have failed in terms of the mainstream culture's norms and values, by giving them alternative routes to achieving status in the eyes of their peers. For example, in school, working-class pupils are likely to fail because they don't have the

Useful synoptic link to education here.

cultural capital, attitudes, skills, etc. needed for success, so they drop out, play truant and misbehave (like the lads in Willis' study). By creating or joining a subculture like this, they can achieve status and 'success', though not in conventional terms.

Relevant knowledge of Cohen's explanation.

Cohen says that working-class boys who have failed in mainstream terms, in education or dead-end jobs, invert the mainstream values and gain status by breaking the rules. So, for example, instead of respecting other people's property they vandalise it. Cohen says the delinquent subculture is characterised by malice and spite.

Appropriate evaluation point here, and useful lead-in to next point.

However, this can be criticised because it assumes that they started off with mainstream values then dropped them when they failed, whereas some would say they never had mainstream values in the first place.

Clear account of Miller – but could bring in concept of 'focal concerns'.

This is similar to Walter B Miller, who argues that the lower class (unskilled, no qualifications, poor, often unemployed) have their own independent subculture that came into being many generations ago as a way of dealing with insecurity and unpleasant, low-paid work. This culture places emphasis on leisure not work as a source of status and identity (since work is menial and badly paid), and emphasises toughness and 'macho' masculinity among men, and a live-for-today attitude. Just by living up to these values, the lower class (especially males) are very likely to get into trouble with the law.

Relevant knowledge of ecological theory, and a brief evaluation of it.

The ecological approach to crime can also help to explain how the working-class offender's background can lead to crime. Sociologists like Shaw, McKay and Burgess argued that certain areas, especially inner city areas, were zones of transition where there were constant population shifts as different groups moved in and out. This meant that there was no fixed culture or clear norms of behaviour, so the area became socially disorganised or anomic, and this led to high rates of crime and other forms of deviance (alcoholism, drug use etc.). However, a lot of inner city areas with high crime rates are actually very stable areas and have clear norms and values, though these may in fact be criminal ones, as Cloward and Ohlin argue.

Better late than never' Good to see a labelling view, even at this late stage. See my comments on Kieran's first paragraph and make the links.

As we have seen, therefore, there are several different explanations of how a working-class background is more likely to lead to crime than say a middle-class one, such as subculture, neighbourhood, and Merton's anomie theory. However, it can also be said that working-class people are no more likely to commit crime (and many are perfectly law-abiding), but just that they are more likely to be labelled by the police. For example, there are more police patrols in working-class neighbourhoods, so working-class offenders are more likely to be noticed.

(25/40)

How to score full marks

This part of the question raises issues about **synoptic links** between, on the one hand, crime and deviance and, on the other hand, **other substantive areas** of the specification – that is, the other topics you have studied except theory and methods. The clue is in the phrase 'social background' – all those things about a person, such as their **family, education, work and leisure, religious beliefs, poverty or wealth, etc.,** that might affect their likelihood of committing crime.

Kieran discusses a number of different approaches quite well, such as anomie, subcultural and ecological theories, but they all have certain things in common – **they assume that the statistics are correct**, and **they owe a lot to Durkheim.** You need to cast your net more widely, and **bring in other kinds of approach.**

Kieran's last paragraph, and my comments on his first one, raise one very different explanation that you should develop – **labelling theory.** Bring in its key concepts – **interaction, definition of the situation, self-fulfilling prophecy** – and apply them to working-class crime (e.g. the idea of a **deviant career**). Start from the idea that the **crime statistics are social constructs** created through labelling/interaction. You could also mention different labelling/law-enforcement agencies (courts, police, probation officers).

Another important approach is **Marxism.** Focus on the way the working class are criminalised, and on the idea that laws are made to benefit the ruling class, not the working class.

A useful distinction for organising this material is between **problem-taking** and **problem-making** approaches to crime. Most of the explanations Kieran has used are problem-takers: they take at face value the statistics that seem to show the problem is working-class crime. Labelling and Marxist approaches are problem-makers: they see the statistics not as straightforward facts, but as outcomes of actions by police, courts, law-makers, the ruling class etc. – and so are more **critical** approaches.

Don't forget ...

Many questions asking for **explanations** of crime and deviance can be answered in terms of a **debate** between Durkheimian theories (anomie, subculture, ecological) and critical theories (labelling, Marxism, feminism etc.) – so make sure you know these and their supporting studies. You can adapt much of this material for use in questions on ethnicity, gender, age, etc., as well as class.

Crime and deviance is a **synoptic** topic, so you need to make links between this topic and sociological theories, methods and other topics you have studied.

Explanations of crime and deviance: Durkheimian or functionalist-inspired theories include anomie theory, subcultural theories and ecological theories. These focus on the offender's background and rely on official statistics.
Traditional Marxists focus on the crimes of the powerful. **New Criminology** draws on both Marxism and labelling theory. **Labelling theory** criticises crime statistics as social constructs and sees deviance as a product of labelling. **Postmodernists** feel that the concept of deviance is obsolete, as there is no longer a single-value system.

Suicide: Positivists see the suicide rate as a social fact – the result of social forces such as lack of integration, so those who are least integrated have the highest suicide rates. **Interpretivists** see suicide as a social construct – a label or meaning rather than a 'fact'. For positivists, the study of suicide shows that sociology is a science – we can quantify events, produce causal laws and make predictions. For interpretivists, the study of suicide shows that features of the social world are simply constructs or interpretations, and require qualitative methods to discover them.

Explanations of the social distribution of crime and deviance: Rates of recorded crime vary between groups – because (1) some groups are more deviant, or (2) law enforcers treat some groups more harshly. Working-class crime appears more common than middle-class crime. Anomie theory explains this as lack of access to legitimate means to achieve. Subcultural theories see it as the acting out of subcultural values. Interactionism focuses on the effects of labelling e.g. by police. Marxism sees it as the result of ruling-class power to criminalise the working class. For control theory, **women** commit less crime because their lives are more constrained. Subcultural theories see much deviance as an exaggerated masculinity. **Blacks** have higher recorded crime rates. Gilroy sees this as the result of discrimination. New Left Realists argue that it stems from marginality, subculture and relative deprivation. **Inner city** areas have higher rates. For ecological theory, this is because they are areas of social disorganisation. The **young** have higher crime rates because of higher participation in gangs, more leisure, fewer legitimate means of success and greater likelihood of being labelled.

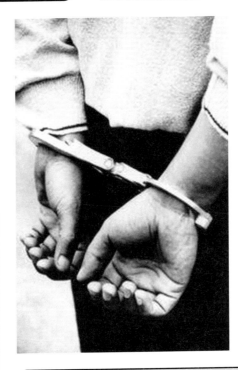

Deviance, power and social control: Marxist, labelling and feminist approaches see deviance as the result of some groups having the power to define the actions of other groups negatively and thereby to control them.

Societal reactions to crime and deviance: The way society reacts to deviance may amplify it. **Interactionists** see societal response to deviance as a cause of further or secondary deviation. The media play a key role in creating moral panics – extreme societal reactions. Cohen's study of mods and rockers shows how **the media** helped to produce a self-fulfilling prophecy of escalating conflict. Other groups – such as police, courts and politicians – also play a part in amplifying a problem. Hall's **neo-Marxist** approach links such societal reactions to the need of capitalism to maintain ruling-class hegemony. **Functionalists** see societal reactions as reinforcing the shared value system when norms have been broken.

Question to try

Answer **both** parts of the question.

Part One

Item A

Participant observation can lead researchers into difficulties. Powdermaker, while researching in the Southern United States, found herself caught up with a lynch mob. She did not know what to do. She concluded that to go to the police would not have helped and would have ruined her research, as would trying to persuade the mob to behave otherwise. She was greatly relieved when the man being hunted, escaped. Not so lucky was Hunter Thompson, who was beaten up by Hell's Angels when he refused to pay them money for the 'privilege' of having 'hung around' observing them.

Adapted from Murray Morison (1986), Methods in Sociology, Longman

(a) Identify and briefly explain **one** advantage and **one** problem in using participant observation to study crime and deviance, apart from those referred to in **Item A**.

[8 marks]

[This part of the question tests your knowledge and understanding of the connections between Crime and Deviance and sociological methods.]

(b) Examine the extent to which the concept of deviance can be used to understand **two or more** areas of social life. [12 marks]

[This part of the question tests your knowledge and understanding of the connections between Crime and Deviance and sociological theory.]

Part Two

(c) 'The idea of power is central to an understanding of crime and deviance.' Assess this view in the light of sociological evidence and arguments. [40 marks]

[This part of the question tests your knowledge and understanding of the connection between Crime and Deviance and other topic(s) that you have studied.]

Examiner's hints

- For **c**, you need both a number of theories and some relevant studies. Conflict theories (Marxism, interactionism, feminism) could be the main focus, but even functionalism has a view of power/authority. Studies of the power of the ruling class to make laws, of the powerful or white-collar criminals to 'get away with it', and of the police, courts and media to label individuals and groups as deviant, are all very relevant.

Answers can be found on pages 91–93.

6 | Stratification and Differentiation

Synoptic assessment

Synoptic assessment is an important part of all A2 exams. Synoptic assessment tests your knowledge and understanding of the subject as a whole, including how the different aspects that you have studied are related. For this reason, the exam paper containing the synoptic assessment can only be taken at the end of your course.

For the AQA's A2 Sociology, **Unit 6 is the synoptic unit**. This offers you a choice of topics: either **Stratification and Differentiation**, or **Crime and Deviance** (see chapter 5). Whichever of these two topics you choose, the questions will test your knowledge and understanding of the links between that topic and three other things:

● other topics you have studied at AS and/or A2

● sociological theories

● sociological methods.

Links between Stratification and Differentiation and other AS/A2 topics

You won't have studied all the other topics in the specification. This does not matter, because the questions are set so that you won't be either advantaged or disadvantaged by studying some topics rather than others. If you have chosen Stratification and Differentiation as your synoptic topic, however, you will need to be able to show that you understand how it links to the other topics that you have already studied in the other AS and A2 units.

There is not space here to list every single link between Stratification and Differentiation and the other ten topics in the specification. Instead, what I have done is to give you examples of some of these links. Thinking about these connections between topics – and trying to think of other ones for the topics you have studied – is a good way to prepare for your exam.

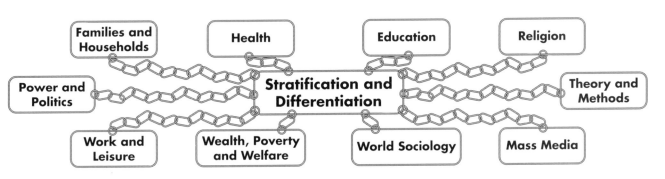

 **Families and Households**

● There are **social class and ethnic** differences in the **structure** of families and households. For example, Willmott and Young found the extended family more common among the working class, and others have found similar patterns among some ethnic minority groups.

● Similarly, there are differences in the **domestic division of labour**, where working-class couples may be more likely to have segregated conjugal roles. While some sociologists argue that **men and women** are becoming **more equal** within the family, **feminists** see the family as perpetuating **women's subordination**. The family remains a major agency of **gender role socialisation**, helping to maintain gender differences. Some would argue that parents and **children** are becoming **more equal** than in the past.

● **State policies** on the family may affect **power relations** in the family, for example by reinforcing **women's** dependence through welfare policies.

● **Working-class** families face more hardship as a result of **industrialisation and urbanisation**, so may be more likely to form extended units for mutual support.

● Similarly, **ethnic groups** may deal with the problems posed by migration by relying on extended kin for assistance. Increasing **family diversity** includes class, ethnic, age and generational differences between households.

● Some social groups are more likely to **divorce** or to have **children outside marriage**, and New Right thinkers see lone-parent families as reproducing an **underclass**.

Health

- A major aspect of the sociology of health is the study of **inequalities in health chances** between social classes, genders and ethnic groups. These are often explained in terms of the health effects of **structural factors** (e.g. in income, housing, leisure opportunities, etc.), or in terms of **cultural differences** between social groups (e.g. how far different **classes** are committed to a lifestyle of short-term hedonism, or different **ethnic** groups hold beliefs that are health-damaging or health-promoting).

- A related area is the extent of inequalities in **access to healthcare** by age, class, ethnicity and gender. **Marxists** see the role of the **medical profession** as upholding class exploitation – by controlling access to sick leave, doctors keep the proletariat at work. **Feminists** see medicine as part of the patriarchal oppression of women; for example, through male control over, and **medicalisation of, childbirth**.

- Rates of **mental illness** differ between **classes, genders and ethnic and age groups**. Some argue that this is a product of the stratification system – the **unemployed**, the **unskilled**, or those facing **racial discrimination**, are more likely to suffer **stress** and other mental health problems.

- **Interpretive** sociologists tend to argue that **stereotyping** and ethnocentric ideas held by **psychiatrists** lead them to mis-interpret what are in fact simply cultural differences in behaviour between different **ethnic groups** as symptoms of mental illness.

Mass Media

- Ownership of the mass media is concentrated in the hands of a few large corporations, themselves often controlled by a few **wealthy individuals**. According to some **Marxists**, media owners control output in the **interests of the capitalist class**, for example by producing **ideology** to persuade the rest of society to accept capitalist rule.

- The mass media's **representations of different groups** – such as social classes, age groups, genders, ethnic minorities, those with disabilities, and gay people – is an aspect of differentiation and stratification. In general, **subordinate groups** in society – those with lower status or less wealth and power – are more likely to be **portrayed in negative ways** compared with those higher up the stratification system. For example, **women** are more likely to be represented as inferior or as victims of their emotions, than men.

- Similarly, according to the Glasgow Media Group, **workers who take strike action** are more likely to be represented as irrational and unreasonable than are employers and managers.

- **News** coverage involves a **hierarchy of credibility**, in which **higher status** individuals are more likely to have their version of events accepted by the media, while **ethnic minorities** may be presented as a threat rather than as victims of discrimination.

Education

- The study of inequalities and differences between **social classes, genders and ethnic groups** has a central place in the sociology of education. Sociologists seek to explain why there is **differential achievement** between these groups. **Material deprivation** and **cultural deprivation** linked to a low-class position have both been identified as reasons for working-class educational failure, as have other class-related factors such as **speech codes** and **cultural capital**.

- **Ethnic differences** can be partly explained by **class** factors, since different ethnic groups tend to be concentrated to some degree in different classes, but **subcultural** differences in socialisation and family structure may also play a part.

- **Gender differences** in educational **achievement** may be the result of wider changes in the **position of women**, such as greater involvement in paid work, while differences in **subject choice** may reflect differences in **gender socialisation and identity**.

Education (continued)

- **Processes within schools**, such as teachers' **labelling** of pupils on the basis of their **class**, **ethnicity** or **gender**, have also been identified as an explanation of differential achievement.
- Education is also seen as **reproducing and legitimising social inequalities**. **Marxists** argue that education perpetuates the class structure and capitalist exploitation, while **feminists** argue that it maintains patriarchy and women's subordination. Both argue that the **hidden curriculum** plays a key role in these processes.

 ## Wealth, Poverty and Welfare

- Wealth, income and poverty are important aspects of the stratification system. Both wealth and income are **unequally distributed** among different social groups. As well as **unskilled manual workers and the unemployed**, groups such as **the elderly**, **children**, some **ethnic minorities** and **women**, are more likely to experience poverty.
- **Relative definitions** see poverty as an aspect of social **inequality** – the inability to participate in the lifestyle that the majority take for granted. **Marxists** explain the existence of both **wealth and poverty** in terms of the nature of **capitalism**, which creates inequalities as a result of exploitation and private property ownership. **Functionalists** see unequal incomes as necessary in a meritocracy to **motivate the talented** to perform the most important jobs.
- **Feminists** see the welfare state and social policy as helping to **perpetuate patriarchy** and women's dependence on men, while **Marxists** tend to see the welfare state as a means of perpetuating capitalism, for example by maintaining the unemployed at subsistence levels so as to hold down the wages of those in work. The **New Right** see an 'over-generous' welfare state as a cause of the underclass' **culture of dependency**.
- **Private welfare provision** (such as private education or healthcare) remains largely the preserve of the higher social classes. **Informal provision**, such as that provided by family members, often means care by **women** for sick or elderly relatives.

 ## Work and Leisure

- **Work** plays a key part in theories of stratification. For **Marxists,** the **exploitation of wage-labourers** by their employers is the basis of the system of class stratification in capitalist society. Exploited workers experience **alienation** and this breeds **class conflict**. Capitalists employ various **surveillance and control** strategies to maintain their grip on the workforce, often using new technology.
- **New technology** may be **creating new classes** and new inequalities, as some gain new skills while others are **de-skilled** or made redundant, and **the unemployed** may come to form an **underclass**.
- Work also has a great influence on our **life-chances**, affecting income, social status, health, education, leisure and the risk of unemployment.
- **Leisure** is strongly linked to stratification. For some professional workers, leisure is an **extension** of work, while unskilled manual workers are more likely to show an **opposition** pattern. **Marxists** see the ruling class as needing to **control working-class leisure**, both to avoid the threat of social **disorder** and potential challenges to their rule, and as a source of profit through **commercialisation** of leisure.
- **Feminists** link **gender differences in leisure** to differences in gender roles and patriarchal domination – women service men's leisure, have fewer leisure opportunities and are excluded from male leisure spaces.
- **Ethnic** and **age** differences also influence leisure patterns. **Postmodernists** argue that **leisure and consumption** are now more important **sources of identity** than class and employment.

Power and Politics

- Many explanations of the **nature and distribution of power** are linked to ideas about social inequality and stratification. **Marxists** argue that political power derives from the economic power of the **capitalist class**, making the economically dominant class the political **ruling class**. **Classical elite theorists** see the superior abilities and organisation of the elite as the basis of their political dominance. **Pluralism** rests on the idea of the **decomposition of class**, creating a more diverse society with many different competing groups.

- The **ideologies and policies of political parties** are traditionally seen as representing **class interests** (e.g. Labour favouring higher welfare state spending to benefit the working class and poor; Conservatives preferring tax cuts for the higher classes). These differences have been linked to **class differences in voting behaviour** – the working class voting Labour and the middle class voting Conservative. Some argue that **class de-alignment** is occurring and the influence of class on voting declining; others argue that class remains important, but that **changes in class structure** are affecting voting behaviour. **Ethnicity and gender** may also influence voting behaviour.

- Some argue that **new social movements** based on gender, ethnicity, sexuality or other status differences are **replacing class and economic issues** as the basis of politics. Others argue that **economic interest groups**, such as big business, remain key players in the political process.

Religion

- **Marxists** argue that religion is an expression of the alienation produced by **class society**. The powerlessness of the poor and oppressed is expressed in the idea of an all-powerful god.

- Religion also serves an **ideological** function, legitimising (justifying) the position of the **ruling class** as ordained by god, masking exploitation and reducing the level of class conflict. **Feminists** see male god-figures, as well as male-dominated priesthoods, as the religious expression of **patriarchal society**.

- Different classes, age groups, genders and ethnic groups have different rates of **religious participation**, and different **religious movements** may appeal to **different classes or ethnic groups**.

- **Sects** often appeal to **the poor** by offering a **theodicy of disprivilege** – a religious justification of their suffering. The encouragement that some sects give to hard work and abstinence means that their members become upwardly mobile, **changing their class position**.

- **Churches** tend to be more conservative and appeal to **higher classes**. In colonised societies, **millenarian movements** may appeal to the native population, sometimes giving rise to nationalist political movements that unite different **ethnic groups** in an anti-colonial struggle.

- Although often a conservative force, religion can act as a force for change, helping to bring **new social classes** to the fore – for example, Calvinist Protestantism was closely linked to the new capitalist class.

World Sociology

- Inequalities between countries or regions such as the 'First World' and the 'Third World' form part of a **global system of stratification**. **Life-chances** for those living in Third World countries are worse than for westerners. For example, in terms of **health**, most Third World countries have lower life expectancy and higher rates of sickness and infant mortality. Similarly, **employment** prospects are generally poorer and wages much lower than in the West, while **environmental damage and degradation** are also usually far more severe in Third World countries.

- Rapid **urbanisation** has left many of **the poor** living in appalling slums and shanty towns. Similarly, Illich and others argue that **education** in Third World countries often

World Sociology (continued)

apes western systems and simply helps **elites** to perpetuate their power and status. **Marxist** and neo-Marxist explanations, such as **dependency theory**, see these inequalities as the product of **exploitation**.

- **Global inequality** is maintained through western domination of international institutions such as the World Bank, **foreign aid**, unequal terms of **trade** and control of investment by western **trans-national corporations**.

- **Feminists** argue that development does not always benefit **women**. For example, **industrialisation** in Third World countries has often relied on women as a **source of cheap labour** for the new mass production industries.

 ## Theory and Methods

- The study of stratification and differentiation raises a number of **methodological issues**. These include how we **define concepts** such as **social class**, **social mobility** or **ethnicity**, and how we should **operationalise** them (i.e. define them in ways that enable us to **measure** them). For example, should we use individuals or households as the unit of analysis when studying social class? Should we use an inter-generational or intra-generational definition of mobility?

- The study of stratification also raises problems of what **methods and sources** to use. **Positivists** and structural sociologists favour quantitative sources that yield large-scale data. This includes census data and other **official statistics**, for example on the occupations, incomes and unemployment rates of different classes, genders, ethnic or age groups. **Interpretivists** and many **feminists** favour more qualitative methods and sources – such as unstructured interviews, participant observation, diaries and life histories – that give validity, enabling the researcher to understand what it is like to be, for example, a member of an oppressed minority group.

- There are also problems in **interpreting the results** of research on stratification: for example, does the finding that rates of mobility have increased mean that we are living in a meritocracy, or simply that there are more jobs at the top?

- The major structural **theories** in sociology – functionalism and Marxism – have views on the nature of social inequality and stratification. The **functionalist** approach to stratification is a **consensus view**, reflecting their idea that inequality is both inevitable and desirable, and that it is based on the different abilities of individuals when judged against society's **shared values**. **Marxist** approaches to stratification reflect the **materialist view** that society is built on economic activity, and that the relationship between the classes engaged in production is one that is based on **exploitation** and gives rise to **class conflict**.

- **Social action theorists**, such as Weber, criticise the Marxist view of stratification for being too **deterministic**, ignoring actors' choices, and for being **one dimensional**, ignoring other social divisions such as gender.

- **Feminism** sees society as based on patriarchal domination of women by men, so that the fundamental social division is one of **gender** rather than class.

- **Marxism** sees itself as a **scientific** account of the **inevitability** of the end of class inequality and the advent of an equal, classless society. However, more recent approaches such as **postmodernism** see the collapse of old 'meta-narratives' (such as the Marxist view of the central importance of class) as society becomes more complex and fragmented, giving rise to **new forms of division and difference**, such as **gender**, **sexuality** and **consumption**.

- All theories of stratification can be accused of **lack of objectivity** and of containing **value judgements** about the desirability or otherwise of inequality. Sociology itself has sometimes influenced **social policy** – on poverty and education, for instance – that has had an impact on the extent of class, gender or ethnic **inequality**.

Answer **both** parts of the question.

Part One

Item A

In an investigation of racial discrimination in employment, Noon (1993) sent matched letters of enquiry to personnel managers at the UK's top 100 companies. The letters were signed by fictitious applicants called Evans and Patel. They were presented as graduate business students about to qualify and who already had relevant experience. Noon's research found that overall the companies were more helpful and encouraging to white candidates. Even among companies that had an equal opportunities policy, nearly half treated the two applicants unequally. Noon's study reveals apparently direct and deliberate discrimination. But equally serious is indirect discrimination.

5

Source: adapted from D. Mason (1995), *Race and Ethnicity in Modern Britain*, Oxford University Press

(a) Identify and briefly explain **two** ways in which one or more of the following may be linked to a person's class position: education; wealth, poverty and welfare; work and leisure.   [8 marks]
[This part of the question tests your knowledge and understanding of the connections between Stratification and Differentiation and other topic(s) that you have studied.]

(b) Using material from **Item A** and elsewhere, examine some of the problems in measuring the extent of discrimination in society.   [12 marks]
[This part of the question tests your knowledge and understanding of the connections between Stratification and Differentiation and sociological methods.]

Part Two

(c) Assess sociological theories of changes in the position of non-manual workers in the class structure.   [40 marks]
[This part of the question tests your knowledge and understanding of the connections between Stratification and Differentiation and sociological theory.]

(a) Identify and briefly explain **two** ways in which one or more of the following may be linked to a person's class position: education; wealth, poverty and welfare; work and leisure.

[8 marks]

EMMA'S ANSWER

One way that education may be linked to a person's class position is through the idea of meritocracy. This is a functionalist idea that a person can earn their own position in the class structure of society by their own efforts, such as by working hard at school and passing their exams. This in turn can lead them to a better job, higher pay, more status etc., so giving them a higher social class position.

> **Good point – the concept of meritocracy links education and class, through the idea of achievement. But Emma should also bring in equal opportunities.**

However, others argue against this, saying that it is not possible or very unlikely for some individuals to do this, such as working class, ethnic minorities etc. (This is also shown in Item A.)

> **Relevant use of the Item, but she could develop it further.**

Poverty may be linked to a person's class position by the fact that if you are working class, especially unskilled working class, you are more likely to be in poverty and part of the 'underclass', e.g. you will most likely be on low pay or even unemployed and living off benefits. This means in all probability you won't be able to have more than the bare necessities.

> **Emma's point about the underclass is potentially useful but she could say a lot more about it.**

(6/8)

How to score full marks

- This part of the question tests your knowledge of **synoptic links** between Stratification and Differentiation and other substantive topics, such as education, poverty etc. Make sure you look for ways to show you can **link your knowledge of the areas specified in the question**.

- **It's OK to use the Item – even if the question doesn't tell you to.** Emma could make more use of it by **explaining** the point she has found in it. You could do this by saying that **'the evidence of discrimination seen in Item A** means an absence of equal opportunities and therefore **shows that employers are not meritocratic'.**

- If you're asked to **'explain'** something (even briefly) you should **aim to develop your points.** Try to **explain the meaning of key terms** and ideas and **show why and how they relate to the question.** You could do this with Emma's point about the **underclass** – define it and link it to a **theory** (e.g. the New Right).

- Another way to develop your answer is to **use examples effectively.** Emma's example on poverty could be better used – e.g. by reference to the notion of **the poverty trap.**

- If you are asked to explain two things, make sure you **write a reasonable amount on each** – unlike Emma, whose answer is a bit brief on poverty.

(b) Using material from **Item A** and elsewhere, examine some of the problems in measuring the extent of discrimination in society.

[12 marks]

EMMA'S ANSWER

Emma makes use of the Item and evaluates some advantages of the method.

The method used in Item A is quite a good one because it can be done quite cheaply just by sending letters or filling in application forms and you can get results from quite a large range, e.g. Noon studied 100 companies, which could have cost quite a lot to send out interviewers for example. It is also good because this gives you an idea of how much discrimination there is, and if you wanted to, it would be quite easy to cover even more companies.

Relevant evaluation again, this time of the disadvantages – plus brief mention of another method.

However, you might face problems with smaller companies, who might not have time or resources to write back to you, so that would give you a false picture. However, you could send out actors (which was done in a TV investigation) to those companies that didn't reply to your letters.

Emma raises some useful points – especially about people not being aware that they had been discriminating or discriminated against – but she doesn't develop them fully.

Another method you could use is to approach members of ethnic minorities to find out how far they had experienced discrimination, but one problem is that they might not know if they had been discriminated against. Alternatively you could even ask white people, e.g. company managers, if they had discriminated against people of a different ethnic group, although obviously they might well lie to you because they were ashamed of their behaviour, or they might not even be aware that they were discriminating.

True – but not very convincing. Does Emma know what these terms mean, or is she just re-cycling a bit of the Item? Probably the latter!

Indirect discrimination is also a problem and sociologists need to consider this when studying the subject, as there is more to the problem than just direct discrimination.

Two useful points – about gender and about quantification – both of which should be taken further.

Another problem is that even if we can measure the extent of racial discrimination, there is still gender discrimination in society and there might be other problems trying to measure this. Also, can these things really be measured and put into numbers? Positivists say they can quantify discrimination into social facts, but interpretivists would say it's a feeling or meaning that can't be turned into mere figures.

7/12

64

How to score full marks

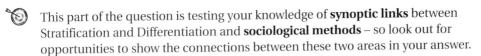

- This part of the question is testing your knowledge of **synoptic links** between Stratification and Differentiation and **sociological methods** – so look out for opportunities to show the connections between these two areas in your answer.

- **Make use of the Item**, as Emma does. You should pick up on **indirect discrimination** from it, too. This is where the routine application of rules has a discriminatory **effect**, even if **no-one intends** to discriminate. You could also bring in related ideas like **institutional racism** here.

- The question is about **discrimination in general**, so why not bring in other forms as well as racial discrimination. Emma briefly mentions **gender** – you could also touch on **age, sexuality or disability**, although you wouldn't have time to discuss each one at length.

- Consider **other methods and sources** as well as the one in the Item – such as **actor tests** (mentioned by Emma), **covert observation**, **official statistics** (e.g. from court cases). Link your discussion to what you know about the strengths and weaknesses of methods – e.g. valid but small-scale qualitative 'interpretative' data versus reliable, representative but superficial quantitative 'positivist' data – and link it to Emma's point about whether people are **aware** of discrimination happening.

Don't forget ...

When asked to **'briefly explain'**, stay focused on the question and aim to develop or expand on some of the issues it raises.

Remember that all parts of the question on Stratification and Differentiation have a synoptic element, so look for ways to **link your knowledge of stratification to the other areas** – sociological theory, sociological methods, and other topics that you have studied during your course.

(c) Assess sociological theories of changes in the position of non-manual workers in the class structure.

[40 marks]

EMMA'S ANSWER

In a meritocratic society, non-manual workers or white-collar workers often have a greater chance of changing their position in the class system as they often have greater abilities such as literacy and more qualifications, which allows them the freedom to move and change their job prospects. Non-manual workers also make up the primary labour market of the dual labour market and therefore have higher paid jobs with more security and greater chances of promotion, which again can result in vertical upward social mobility.

Non-manual workers also have more skills to offer as the service sector of the economy takes over from the industrial sector such as factories, coal mining etc. Non-manual workers are therefore at less risk from de-skilling compared to manual workers. For example, there has been a big drop in the number of jobs in the motor car industry as a result of new technological innovations.

However, more recently with the introduction of information technology and computers into offices there has been a big fall in the number of non-manual jobs that are available, and this has had a number of different effects. Those who have lost their jobs have become downwardly mobile into the ranks of the unemployed or underclass, whereas those who have kept their jobs may have improved their prospects, especially if they have the skills needed to work with the new information technology. Duncan Gallie found that those non-manual workers who were already the most qualified or skilled were the ones most likely to get access to training and further skills, while those with less skill who needed the training most, got less opportunities to train. So there was a growing gap or division in non-manual work as a result of the new technology.

Women are found concentrated in non-manual work, but mainly at the lower levels (women's earnings are generally about 80 per cent of men's). They are more likely to have the routine office jobs, whereas men are more likely to be found as supervisors or managers. Rosemary Crompton found that up to the age of about 30, men and women in office work had about the same position, but after 30 men started to move ahead, getting more promotions. This also fits with Gallie's findings about training, since men get more training chances and this brings promotion. Also,

women are discriminated against by male bosses who think they will leave to have babies, so are less likely to give them promotions or put them into key roles in the organisation. One study of banking and finance found that although 70 per cent of clerical workers were women, only 14 per cent of top grade managers were women.

It is also said that there has been a feminisation of clerical work. In the 19th century, clerks were male and they held a high status position in the workplace. But as companies got bigger, so did their offices and gradually more and more women came into this field, doing the routine jobs that big offices have (because of division of labour), such as filing, typing etc. Because women are seen as having a primary role as carer not as breadwinner (and also may see themselves in this way), it was possible to pay them less. As the numbers of women white-collar workers grew, this pushed wages down, so that by the late 20th century, routine office work often paid less than some manual jobs.

However, Lockwood found when studying clerical workers that they still had better status situations than manual workers, e.g. people looked up to them more than to labourers or factory workers. This is partly because they have reflected status from working closer to their bosses (e.g. in the same office, maybe on first name terms etc., unlike a shopfloor worker on the assembly line). Also, as mentioned at the beginning, they have more security and don't get made redundant as much as manual workers.

However, in an industry such as banking, in the 1990s over 80,000 jobs were lost, mainly because of new technology (e.g. telephone banking, cash points) and mergers etc. Non-manual workers these days are more likely to go on strike, as Marx predicted with his theory of proletarianisation.

Contrary to proletarianisation, some sociologists argue that embourgeoisement is taking place, where the affluent (well paid) section of manual workers are joining the middle class, for example taking on their attitudes and values, voting Conservative rather than traditional working-class Labour voting, buying their own homes etc. All these things are seen as traditionally middle class, so this shows that the non-manual or middle class are on the increase. However, Goldthorpe and Lockwood disproved this theory back in the 1960s with their famous Affluent Worker study of Luton car workers who were well paid but who had not become middle class e.g. they still voted Labour.

Some more useful material on gender. Some feminist concepts like patriarchy would also help.

Emma could refer to work and market situation as well as status situation.

Emma seems to be using this to evaluate Lockwood – a good idea, but she needs to spell out the implications more fully. Proletarian-isation is a key idea and needs a paragraph to itself.

Embourgeoisement is about changes in the working class, not the middle/non-manual class – so not really relevant here. Cut it and write about proletarianisation instead!

> The reserve army of labour has been on the increase, as there are more and more part-time positions being created in non-manual work and service industries. This means that many non-manual workers are competing for these jobs and this pushes down wages, which advantages the employers.
>
> Overall the position of non-manual workers is fluctuating in the class system, depending on whereabouts in the system they are.

Potentially relevant, but might go better in an earlier paragraph.

A bit thin for a conclusion!

25/40

How to score full marks

- Write a **proper introduction**. You can briefly **interpret what the question is about** and **raise some of the key issues** you're going to discuss. Obviously this means you will need to **plan your answer** first.

- Remember that **this is a synoptic topic** and the **wording of the question makes it clear** that the **link is to sociological theory** – so it would be a good idea to refer to some relevant theories from the start, instead of leaving it for several paragraphs, as Emma does.

- **General theories of society** – such as **Marxism, Weberianism and feminism** – all have something to say about this question. For instance, you could briefly outline Marx's central ideas and then apply them to the issues raised by the growth of non-manual jobs.

- A key debate is whether **proletarianisation** has occurred. This needs explaining and linking to **Marxism**, e.g. using **Braverman's** work. You could use **Lockwood** to criticise this, linking his ideas to **Weber's** general views on class.

- Other issues you could examine include **fragmentation** or **polarisation** of the middle class into two or more separate classes, the impact of **universal education** (e.g. clerks' literacy is no longer a special skill), **class consciousness and trade union membership** among non-manual workers, and (as Emma does) the **feminisation** of white-collar work.

- **'Non-manual workers' is a big category** (the majority of workers are now non-manual). Emma looks mainly at routine **clerical** workers, mentions **managers** now and then, but says nothing about **professionals** (doctors, teachers, lawyers etc.). You need to discuss **all three**.

- **Beware** of using material on the **embourgeoisement** debate – it's about changes in the **working** class rather than among non-manual workers.

- Write a **proper conclusion.** An essay involves developing an argument, so you need to show at the end where this argument has led you to. You could **re-state the key changes and/or the key theories** you have discussed, **and make a final judgement on their importance**.

Don't forget ...

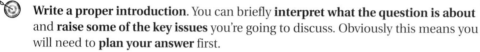

Essays are extended pieces of reasoning, so it's vital that you give them a **clear structure**. This means you have **to plan** before writing.

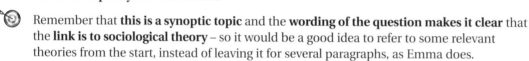

When you answer questions that ask about sociological theories, make sure you **outline, explain and assess some!** Theories should provide the basic framework of your answer.

Key points to remember

Occupation and social class: Most measures of social class use occupation to allocate individuals to classes. For example, the **Registrar-General's classification** of social class is used in official government **censuses**. Such classifications are useful because occupation is a fairly **good indicator of life-chances** such as health, educational level and income. But occupational classifications have their **problems**: classifying those who don't have jobs (over half the population), such as housewives or the unemployed, is difficult; women are often classified according to their husband's occupation; they ignore property ownership; it is difficult to evaluate the skill level of jobs objectively.

Differences in life-chances: The concept of life-chances refers to **the likelihood of enjoying scarce desirable resources or opportunities**, such as a good education, access to healthcare, well-paid employment, and so on. In stratification systems, higher placed groups generally enjoy better life-chances than those lower down. Thus the middle **class** are more likely than the working class to have higher educational qualifications and secure, satisfying jobs, to live in good-quality housing, and to lead long and healthy lives. **Ethnic** groups, **age** groups and **genders** can also be stratified in these ways – for example, black people on average earn less than whites and women earn less than men.

Social mobility: Mobility is **movement up or down the class structure**. It can be **inter-generational** (comparing parents' and children's class positions) or **intra-generational** (measuring changes in an individual's position during their working life). The rate of mobility is affected by factors such as **changes in the occupational structure** (e.g. an increase in the number of middle-class jobs) and moves towards **meritocracy** (e.g. more equal opportunities for talented individuals to move into higher positions). There are **problems measuring mobility**: e.g. whether to use an inter- or intra-generational measure; many studies ignore women's mobility, which may be different from men's; the status of jobs changes over time, making them hard to compare.

Theories of stratification: In **Marx's two-class model**, capitalist owners of the means of production exploit the proletariat, or working class. This gives rise to class conflict and ultimately a socialist revolution and the creation of a classless society. Critics argue that this is deterministic, and that it ignores other kinds of inequality (e.g. gender and ethnic); as well as the existence of more than two classes. **Weber** sees **several classes**, including a non-manual middle class and skilled and unskilled manual classes based on differences in market situation. He also identifies two non-class forms of inequality: **status** (prestige or social honour) and **power** (the ability to achieve one's goals even against opposition). **Feminists** argue that society is male-dominated, or **patriarchal**. Radical feminists see men as the cause of women's oppression; whereas Marxist feminists argue that capitalism is the prime beneficiary. **Functionalists** see inequality as inevitable and beneficial: unequal rewards motivate the most able to perform the most important jobs. They regard modern society as **meritocratic** – based on equal opportunity to achieve.

Changes in the class structure: Marx predicted that the proletariat (working class) would expand and unite as capitalism grew, but the 1950s **embourgeoisement** thesis argued that growing prosperity was making the working class more middle class. However, **Goldthorpe and Lockwood** found no evidence of affluent workers taking on middle-class values, lifestyles or voting behaviour. Others argue that the working class is **internally divided**, e.g. by skill levels. Some claim that there is an **underclass** trapped below the working class, in poorly-paid, insecure jobs, in which ethnic minorities are over-represented. The **New Right** argue that **welfare dependency** is a major cause of the underclass. **Marxists** argue that the middle class are becoming **proletarianised** – sinking into the working class – through deskilling, but the Weberian **Lockwood** argues that even routine white-collar workers still have a different market, work and status situation from manual workers. Some argue that both the working and the middle classes are becoming increasingly **fragmented**.

Question to try

Answer **both** parts of the question.

Part One

Item A

According to Parkin, the occupational hierarchy is the 'backbone' of the stratification system of modern societies. Occupational position is a central cause of differences in life-chances, lifestyle and political outlook. Status is important, but one's status is largely a result of one's class position.

Nevertheless, there are several problems involved in using occupation to define and   5
measure social class. Class position should be thought of as related to, but not the same as, occupation. However, even though there are several reasons why occupation is unsatisfactory as a sole indicator of class position, it is the most useful single measure available.

Source: adapted from N. Abercrombie *et al*, *Contemporary British Society*, 2nd edition (Polity Press) 1994.

(a) Briefly discuss some of the problems of using occupation to measure social class.

[8 marks]

[This part of the question tests your knowledge and understanding of the connections between Stratification and Differentiation and sociological methods.]

(b) With reference to material from any part of the course, examine the extent to which social class exerts an influence on different aspects of people's lives.   [12 marks]

[This part of the question tests your knowledge and understanding of the connections between Stratification and Differentiation and other topic(s) that you have studied.]

Part Two

(c) Assess the view that stratification is both inevitable and beneficial to individuals and society.   [40 marks]

[This part of the question tests your knowledge and understanding of the connections between Stratification and Differentiation and sociological theory.]

Examiner's hints

● For **(c)**, you need to recognise that this is a functionalist view and you should link it to the general functionalist theory of society. You can outline it using Davis and Moore, and you should evaluate it using arguments from other perspectives such as Marxism or feminism, and/or by using the work of writers such as Tumin. You should also examine both the 'inevitability' of stratification and consider whether it is 'beneficial' and, if so, to whom. You could also draw on evidence from studies of kibbutzim, the former Soviet Union etc.

Answers can be found on pages 94–96.

Answers to Questions to try

1 Power and Politics

🎯 How to score full marks

1 (a) Some sociologists argue that an equal or classless society – such as Marxists predict, or such as socialist and communist parties strive for – is impossible to achieve. This is for several reasons. Firstly, elite theorists such as Mosca and Michels argue that elite rule, and therefore some form of hierarchy, is inevitable. For example, Michels claimed to have discovered a scientific law of political organisation, which he called the 'iron law of oligarchy'. Oligarchy means rule by a few, and Michels and other elite theorists argue that a minority elite will always be able to dominate the non-elite majority. Mosca argues that this is because the elite have several advantages over the masses – being a smaller group, they are more cohesive and easier to organise than the masses, and they can conspire together more easily to keep themselves in a dominant position.

A second reason why some argue that equality or classlessness is impossible comes from functionalist sociologists who argue that it is essential to ensure that the most important roles are filled by the most able and talented individuals. This is true in all societies, but it is even more so in modern industrial societies. This kind of society relies on science and advanced technology, so it is vital that those occupying key positions have knowledge and expertise. In order to get the most able people to perform these vital roles, society must offer them higher rewards to encourage them to train and prepare. So unequal rewards are inevitable and necessary to the smooth running of modern society.

> **Examiner's comment**
> Two suitable reasons, both clearly explained.
> It would also be legitimate to use a different reason from another elite theorist such as Pareto.

1 (b) Although it is generally possible to identify political parties as having some sort of ideology, there are several reasons why party policies and actions (e.g. when in government) are not governed solely by their ideology. Some reasons are to do with the ideology itself, while other reasons result from other factors apart from ideology affecting policies.

Firstly, an ideology is often a set of quite general, even woolly, beliefs (in equality, individual freedom etc.) and there may be disagreements within the party as to how to translate them into particular policies. For example, members may disagree as to whether 'equality' means a policy of equal incomes, or one of equal opportunities to earn unequal rewards. Also, as parties are generally loose coalitions of groups, not everyone may subscribe to the official ideology. Once in power, they may ignore it where they can. Similarly, parties may change their ideology in order to win power if they find that their existing ideology makes them unpopular with the electorate.

Pluralists argue that one reason why ideology does not always dictate policies is that, especially when in government, parties find themselves under more pressure both from a variety of pressure groups and from public opinion. They have to please people other than their own activists, especially if they want to retain popularity and win the next election. If they are in a coalition government, they may have to 'tone down' their own ideology in order to reach compromise with other parties in the government.

Marxists such as Miliband argue that democratic socialist parties, once in government, find themselves having to implement pro-capitalist policies. Even though their ideology is anti-capitalist, they are often too weak to withstand pressure from the capitalist class and its allies in the 'establishment' – the top civil servants, military, judiciary, etc.

Elite theorists may argue that ideology is just a tool to use to manipulate the masses and retain power. For example, Stalin cynically used communist ideology to mobilise the masses to fight wars, make sacrifices to industrialise the country etc.

Thus there are numerous reasons why ideology, though having some influence on party policies and actions, does not dictate them.

> **Examiner's comment**
> Lots of good reasons examined: the vagueness of ideologies; parties as coalitions; the need to win popularity with voters; Marxist, elitist and pluralist arguments.

2 It is said that today we live in a democracy, in which there is majority rule. Yet at the same time many argue that the majority are increasingly powerless, for example with the spread of globalisation, power now lies in the headquarters of big trans-national companies, not in elected parliaments. On the other hand, we have recently seen devolution – the spreading of power to make decisions and laws away from Westminster to the Scottish Parliament and the Welsh and Northern Ireland Assemblies. Two sociological theories in particular might agree with the view in the question – Marxists and elite theorists.

Marx argued that power comes from ownership of the means of production. This resulted in a class society in which economic power gave a minority – the capitalist class or bourgeoisie – political power through control of the state, making the economically dominant class also the political ruling class. Orthodox Marxists today continue this argument. Miliband argues that through control of the state, the ruling class is able to protect private property, control the working class and preserve capitalism. Capitalist interests are also protected by the fact that those in command of the state – senior civil servants, generals, judges, etc. – are themselves from highly privileged backgrounds socially and educationally (public school, Oxbridge, family ties to big business, etc.), as Stanworth and Giddens show. Thus a small group of people, with close ties to the capitalist class, run the state in the interests of capitalism.

Elite theories agree with the Marxist view that power is held by a small, cohesive minority group. They argue that power is in the hands of a minority, but they refer to it as an elite rather than a ruling class. This indicates that, unlike Marxists, they do not necessarily see political power coming from economic power – it can have other bases, such as psychological characteristics of the elite (e.g. Pareto's lions and foxes) or organisational skills. Unlike Marxists, elite theorists see society as inevitably unequal and they do not see an end to minority rule with a socialist revolution. Instead, one elite simply replaces another, and this 'circulation of elites' (Pareto) endlessly repeats itself. Despite their differences, however, some writers, like Mills, have combined elements of Marxism and elite theory, arguing there is a 'power elite' made up of three inter-related elites (business, military and political), whose members move easily from one to the other.

In extreme versions of both Marxism and elite theory, only the tiny minority at the top holds power, but in some other versions, the majority are capable of gaining some power or influence, even though ultimate power rests with the elite/ruling class. For example, neo-Marxists or structuralist Marxists, such as Poulantzas, argue that the state has relative autonomy (independence) from the ruling class, so it doesn't always do its bidding and acts like a 'referee' between the working class and capitalist class. As a result, the working class can occasionally make some gains and win reforms through trade union action or through electing a 'reformist' government (e.g. the Labour government of 1945). This suggests that power is not entirely concentrated, but Poulantzas argues that the basic function of the state is to serve the ruling class, and so these reforms are often just concessions by the ruling class to buy off opposition and prevent more serious challenges to their power.

Similarly, Gramsci argues that within the framework of capitalist society, different groups and classes struggle for influence and although the capitalist class remains the ruling class, they are forced to make concessions and alliances with other groups to maintain their hegemony (society's acceptance of their moral leadership or right to rule, as opposed to rule through pure force). Therefore, the ruling class have to some extent to share power if they want to keep power.

At the other extreme from Marxism and elite theory is classical pluralism. This argues that modern societies are no longer ruled by a minority (i.e. a ruling class or elite) acting in their own interests. They have instead become representative democracies in which indirectly (i.e. through their representatives) the majority now rule. Power is thus dispersed or diffused throughout society. In this view, put forward by Dahl, society is no longer a two-class society described by Marx, but made of many competing groups, all of whom are able to exert some influence on decision making, and who often end up compromising, so that decisions reflect the interests of several groups, not just one dominant group. This is similar to Dahrendorf's idea that modern society has seen the 'decomposition of capital' and the 'decomposition of labour' (the two main classes in Marx's view). That is, they have broken down into several groups with sometimes conflicting interests (e.g. capital has split into shareholders and managers) and so no longer have overriding power. However, one version of this view is that of Burnham's 'managerial revolution', that the managers, experts and bureaucrats who now run the economy and government have become a new minority ruling class, ruling in their own interests as capitalists did previously – so power remains concentrated, but in new hands.

Another criticism of classical pluralism comes from Lukes, who argues that we need to examine the different 'faces' of power itself. To understand who rules, we must look not only at decision making, as Dahl claims, but non-decision making or agenda setting (the issues that are not even discussed) and shaping decisions (where people's viewpoints are shaped by the dominant ideology and things such as the private ownership of wealth are made to seem inevitable or natural). The last two of these three 'faces of power' suggest that there is an elite or ruling class able to use ideological and agenda-setting power to their own benefit.

Females make up a majority of the population, yet men dominate the 'public sphere' (state, economy etc.) and the positions of power, status and reward. Feminists argue that in patriarchal society, men hold power in their own interests, while women are either confined to the 'private sphere' (family) or enter the public sphere only as subordinates. Their concerns are often ignored by power-holders, as Dobash and Dobash's study of domestic violence shows. While radical and Marxist feminists argue that it will take a major upheaval to change this, liberal feminists take something of a pluralist view and argue that a diffusion of power is beginning to occur with gradual reforms which are starting to equalise the position of the sexes and give women access to power. For example, Britain now has its largest number of female MPs and several other countries have even higher proportions of women in parliament.

To counter these criticisms, elite pluralism developed, with the idea that although many groups compete for influence, some groups have more access to power than others. This suggests that power is more concentrated than Dahl originally believed, but still retains the idea that it is possible for different groups to gain some influence, even if unequally.

The classical pluralist view of power has been criticised as naïve. Left critics (e.g. Marxists) argue that pluralists are wrong in thinking that power is evenly dispersed to all groups in society, and that the state is impartial; instead they argue that business interests tend to dominate the state. And they argue that pluralism neglects Lukes' other 'faces of power'. The Right argue that veto groups (such as the unions under previous Labour governments) have undue influence over decisions.

As we have seen, some sociologists – like Marxists, elite theorists, and radical and Marxist

feminists – tend to argue that power is concentrated in the hands of a minority and used for their own interests. However, some versions of Marxism accept that the ruling class can only maintain its position by making some concessions, so their power is not absolute or totally concentrated. At the other end of the spectrum of views, classical pluralists see a dispersal or diffusion of power throughout society, so that no minority group dominates and all have broadly equal influence. However, from within pluralism, the elite pluralists argue that this influence is not equal and that some have a bigger voice than others, although they still hold that none can monopolise power. Thus if democracy means power is held by the majority, many sociological perspectives would reject the view that modern societies are truly democratic.

> **Examiner's comment**
> This is a **well-balanced** answer, with a range of arguments for and against the view that power in modern societies is concentrated in the hands of a minority. A good, **thorough knowledge** of Marxism, elite theory, pluralism, the managerial revolution thesis, feminism etc. – including some of the different variants of these (e.g. orthodox and neo-Marxism, classical elite theory and Mills' 'power elite', classical and elite pluralism, radical, Marxist and liberal feminism). Many of these are **evaluated** either by reference to evidence (e.g. devolution, trans-national companies, Stanworth and Giddens, Dahrendorf, Dobash and Dobash), or by criticisms from other perspectives. There is an appropriate **conclusion** linking the main arguments back to the question and reflecting on what these mean for the idea of democracy.

3 There has been much debate about the role of pressure groups in the political process. Some sociologists, such as pluralists, argue that pressure groups are an essential feature of modern representative democracies, while others see them as a threat to democracy, using their power to 'hold the country to ransom' until their demands are met.

Pluralists argue that, in modern societies, political parties alone are inadequate for representing everyone's needs and interests. This is because society is made up of a plurality of different groups – consumer groups, producer groups etc. – and because elections only take place every four or five years, so citizens cannot express their views very often through their vote.

As a result of the diversity of views and groups in society, pressure groups have come into existence. Pressure groups differ from parties in that parties seek to govern the country, i.e. to exercise power and put their policies into practice. They do this by fighting and winning elections. Pressure groups don't seek to govern the country, but simply to influence the government or other decision makers on issues that they are concerned about. Another difference is that parties have a wide range of policies (on education, health, the economy, law and order, etc.), whereas pressure groups are only concerned with a limited range of issues. For example, CPAG is concerned only with child poverty and related issues, not with defence policy, whereas a party must have something to say about everything in order to appeal to the largest number of voters.

Sociologists identify two different types of pressure groups. Promotional pressure groups seek to promote a particular 'cause' (such as the environment, animal welfare etc.) and membership is generally open to anyone who agrees with them (e.g. Greenpeace, the RSPCA). The other type is protective pressure groups, or interest groups. They represent the sectional interests of a particular group of people (e.g. farmers, teachers, small businesses) and membership of the pressure group usually depends on being a member of the relevant section of the population. Interest groups are very often concerned mainly with economic issues.

From a pluralist perspective, Almond argues that pressure groups contribute to the democratic process partly in conjunction with parties. Pressure groups express the interests and demands of particular sections of society and try to influence the parties. Parties in turn incorporate aspects of the pressure groups' demands into their policies and manifestos as a way of winning the votes of those who back the pressure groups. Then, in government, they enact policies to meet some of these demands. Pressure groups also help parties and government to formulate policies. Since the pressure group is often more knowledgeable about a particular issue than a party is, it can help by providing information, research and proposals for policies. (In a way, the pressure group is a specialist in its own field, whilst the party is more general.) Also, between elections pressure groups are important in bringing issues to the attention of government by campaigning, protesting, lobbying MPs, etc. This enables government to recognise and respond to new needs in society. Even people who

voted for the government may not agree with all its policies, and pressure-group activity allows citizens to campaign to change particular policies on specific issues.

Another important feature of the pluralist view is that the state acts as a kind of honest broker or referee between the competing interests of different pressure groups in society. As a result, no single interest group gets all its own way or is able to influence decisions all the time. This means that many different individuals and groups can have some say in decision making, which is thus good for democracy.

However, not all sociologists accept this view of pressure groups. New Right critics such as Brittan argue that pressure groups contribute to government overload, increased taxation and weak economic performance. Because governments want to get re-elected, they court popularity by giving in to pressure group demands. This usually involves spending more money, pushing up taxation and draining the productive sector of the economy. They also argue against 'corporatism', and are especially opposed to trade union influence on government, as in the Labour governments of the 1960s–1970s.

Others argue that more wealthy groups can afford ways of exerting more pressure, e.g. by funding parties, sponsoring MPs, spending large budgets on advertising, even bribery, as ways of influencing decisions. Other critics argue that not all pressure groups wield equal influence on government, and that some groups have no real pressure to exert. For example, pensioners cannot go on strike or cause the value of the currency to collapse by shifting their investments out of the country, so they are less likely to be listened to than are trade unions or wealthy capitalists.

Elite pluralist writers like Wyn Grant distinguish between 'insider' and 'outsider' pressure groups in terms of how much they are listened to by government. 'Insiders' like the BMA or CBI are likely to have their views taken into account by politicians or civil servants and be seen as respectable, reasonable etc., whereas 'outsiders' like CND may be seen as extreme, unrealistic etc. Insiders are more likely to share the values of the political elite, and maybe also the same privileged background (and so can use the 'old boy network'). However, groups can shift from one to the other – for example, Margaret Thatcher started to treat the unions as outsiders, and today some environmentalist groups may now be becoming insiders. But this may mean that their leaders have to screen out more radical demands coming from their members, since they believe that these will prove too extreme and they will be seen as irresponsible by government, thus losing influence. If so, this means that some interests and views are not getting through to government, which would seem undemocratic. This may, in turn, lead outsider groups to demonstrations, direct action and even illegal action (e.g. riots, terrorism), as they are unable to get their views across by other means.

Marxists in general have not written much about pressure groups, but they do not see capitalist societies like Britain as true democracies where the government represents the interests of the majority. Instead, it serves minority capitalist interests. So a Marxist approach would agree that different groups have different influence, but would go on to argue that this is the result of capitalist groups owning the means of production, the decisive advantage from a Marxist perspective.

Finally, some see the role of pressure groups as undergoing change. Grant argues that since the 1970s the number of groups has greatly increased, so more interests are now represented. Big economic interest groups like the TUC and CBI have lost some influence, and more groups use direct action than before (e.g. roads protesters, farmers' blockades of ports). They now also put pressure on other decision makers, not just central government (e.g. the EU, Scottish Parliament, the courts) and on the public (e.g. to boycott certain products).

Overall, then, pluralists argue that pressure groups play a vital part in maintaining democracy by providing a means of influencing decisions to all who wish to do so. Others are less convinced, seeing them as giving some groups privileged access to decision makers, overloading government or providing capitalists with a backdoor to power behind the democratic façade.

Examiner's comment
A well-organised, well-argued answer. Good idea to put the role of pressure groups into the **context of pluralism** – the relationship between PGs, parties and government is well explained. A good knowledge of **relevant material on PGs** is shown (e.g. insider versus outsider groups, protective and promotional groups). Lots of useful **examples** of actual PGs throughout the essay show the ability to apply sociological ideas to the real world. Effective **evaluation** comes from good use of **alternative approaches** to PGs (e.g. from the New Right, Marxism, and elite pluralists). There is **up-to-date material** about pressure groups today, and a brief but sharp **conclusion**.

2 Religion

🎯 How to score full marks

1 (a) Statistics on religious practices have often been used to measure religiosity. These include statistics on practices such as church attendance and baptism (as in Item A), as well as figures on other rituals such as church weddings, ordinations for the priesthood etc. However, one problem is unreliability. For example, accurate counting and comparing of the numbers attending Church of England services on Easter Sunday may not be possible. Who is to do the actual counting at each church and who is to report and add the figures together for the country as a whole? Also, even if the counting is accurate, attendance on one day of the year may not be reproduced on another, nor do all churches count attendance in the same way.

A second problem is validity – can statistics tell us anything about the true meaning of these practices for those involved? For example, is 'going to church' the same thing as 'being a Christian'? For many it is not – surveys show that many believe that 'you don't have to go to church to be a good Christian'. So the figures may only measure a certain kind of religiosity – one involving belief in the need to go to church. This problem is made worse because the number holding to this kind of Christianity may be declining while at the same time the number still seeing themselves as Christian may not. A good example is the Victorian era, when church-going was required for middle-class respectability, more or less regardless of personal belief – making it difficult to conclude that high levels of church-going (4–5 times higher than now) meant high levels of religious faith.

> **Examiner's comment**
> Problems of reliability and validity of statistics on religious practices are both well explained – especially validity.

1 (b) There are a number of problems in trying to define religion. The first is the great variety of things that people see as being religion. For example, as Item A shows, definitions such as Tylor's involve belief in supernatural spirits, yet it can be argued that some religions (e.g. Buddhism) do not have this belief. And some writers would argue that simply belief in the existence of spirits is not enough – there has to be belief in their power to influence human affairs.

There is also the problem of defining religion separately from magic and science. Magic is often defined as an attempt to influence events using supernatural powers, but much 'religious' behaviour falls into this category, especially prayers asking for God to intervene. Also, how do we classify beliefs such as the ancient Greek idea that everything was made up of tiny particles called 'atoms'? We can now prove their existence, but the Greeks had to accept the belief on faith alone – would that make it religious or scientific?

Other definitions focus on behaviour rather than beliefs. For example, Durkheim sees religion as a collective ritual. Durkheim's definition is functionalist – religion is something that functions to cement individuals together by making them recognise they are all part of something greater than themselves and to which they owe duties. For Durkheim, 'religion is society, but society transfigured' into an idealised version that individuals can understand. One problem with this definition is that it is too wide – almost anything can be a religion so long as it involves collective rituals that bind people together, from political movements (e.g. nationalism, with its flags and anthems) to football teams (likewise!). Also, it works better for simpler societies where everyone shares the same religion, but modern or complex societies often contain two or more religions, which both bind believers together into communities and simultaneously cause conflict, as in Northern Ireland, Palestine/Israel etc., or the religious wars in 16th–17th century Europe.

Another feature of Durkheim's definition is that religion is institutionalised – that is, a shared practice governed by clear norms. But postmodernists argue that individuals now construct their own religions, by picking and mixing beliefs and practices as they choose, in a de-institutionalised way.

To conclude, there are many problems defining religion: some are too broad, such as functional ('inclusive') definitions, whereas others, based usually on beliefs, may be too narrow or have difficulties deciding exactly which beliefs 'count'. Similarly, institutional definitions ignore many practices, especially today, that participants see as religious.

> **Examiner's comment**
> A range of problems examined, focusing on different aspects of religion, such as belief, practice and institutionalisation.

2 Many sociologists argue that religion acts as a conservative force in society, preventing or inhibiting change. For example, for different reasons both functionalists and Marxists see religion as maintaining the status quo and upholding the existing social structure. Nevertheless, there is plentiful evidence that religion may sometimes act as a powerful force for social change.

Probably the best known upholder of this view is Max Weber. In his study, 'The Protestant Ethic and the Spirit of Capitalism', Weber argues that it was Protestantism, and especially Calvinism, that brought about modern capitalism. Weber was concerned to argue against the materialist or Marxist view that only material factors can bring about social change (such as the birth of capitalism). He argues that if we look at material conditions, India and China were more advanced than western Europe, yet it was in the West not the East that modern capitalism first arose. This was because of the influence of Calvinistic beliefs on people's actions.

According to Weber, Calvin's ideas of predestination – the notion that God's will was unknowable and the idea of 'this-worldly asceticism' – produced in believers the kind of behaviour that led to capitalism. Calvinists believed that God had predestined every soul to be either saved (one of the 'Elect' or chosen), or not. However, God's will was unknowable (e.g. by priests, the church etc.) and unalterable by human actions (such as prayers). This created an 'unprecedented inner loneliness' and 'salvation panic' among believers – since they did not know whether they were saved and in any case could do nothing to earn salvation (God having already decided who was saved). However, the Calvinist belief in 'this-worldly asceticism' offered a kind of solution. It refers to the idea that God can call us to a 'vocation', or work, to serve Him, not only by being 'other-worldly' (e.g. joining a monastery and withdrawing from this world), but by working systematically at a job or career. So the Calvinists, to distract themselves from their salvation anxieties, threw themselves into systematic business activity, renouncing leisure and consumption. The result of this rational, systematic work and abstention from consuming was that they rapidly accumulated wealth and spread the spirit of modern capitalism – systematic effort for its own sake. This is, in fact, similar to Marx's view that capitalism involves 'production for production's sake, accumulation (of wealth) for accumulation's sake'. Calvinism thus brought modern capitalism into being.

However, Weber's thesis has been widely criticised. Many Marxist and other historians have argued that in fact capitalism pre-dates Calvinism so logically cannot be the result of it. Some, such as John Foster, argue that in fact Calvinism was really an ideology by which early capitalists controlled their apprentices and servants. However, whatever the truth of these criticisms, Weber was very well aware that religion alone was insufficient and that there had to be a certain level of development of economic, political, legal and other institutions before capitalism could take off even in the west. Weber was also aware that some religions can act as a barrier to economic and social change, and he argued that Hinduism, by legitimating the caste system, prevented change in India.

The debate about millenarian movements also raises issues about the role of religion in social change. Some such as Cohn ('Pursuit of the Millennium') argue that these are irrational utopian movements that cannot bring about real change. However, Marxist writers such as Worsley and Hobsbawm argue that, although millenarian movements may be 'unrealistic', they are often the precursors of secular political movements, such as nationalism and trade unionism, and they provide experience in political skills of organisation, leadership etc. Indirectly, therefore, this type of religion may give rise to other movements that can bring about change. This reflects the Marxist view that religion is 'the sigh of the oppressed creature, the heart of a heartless situation'. In other words, the oppressed often use religion to give voice to their feelings and demands and, though religion cannot achieve a better society, it can lead to political movements for change.

Equally, however, religion may act as a barrier to change. For example, it is argued that pentecostalist and evangelical sects in Brazil encourage the poor not to rebel, and to blame their misfortune on their sins rather than on society/capitalism. This reflects Weber's idea of a 'theodicy of disprivilege' – religions offer an explanation of misfortune or apparent injustice. One factor therefore in whether a religion promotes change is the nature of its beliefs and how it explains misfortune and what solutions it proposes. Some religions preach resignation to fate (such as Hinduism) and thus discourage believers from taking action to change things, whereas others call on believers to act against injustice in the here and now (e.g. the Islamic idea of 'jihad' or holy war). The important point here is that we need to consider the particular type of religion, its followers and the social circumstances – it's too broad to just talk about religion in general as if it were a single thing.

A similar argument is used by McGuire. She suggests that the potential of a religion to bring change depends on a number of factors, such as the specific beliefs of the religion. For example, a religion that encourages its members to turn their backs on the world may be less likely to promote change. We could add factors like the social background of its members – if they are rich and highly placed they may be more attracted to religions that justify their privileges than religions that seek to overthrow the existing hierarchy.

We also need to consider what we mean by social change. Marxists and others often mean 'change in a certain direction', that is towards a classless or at least a modern society. On this view, religion is often seen as conservative, because it often upholds 'traditional' or pre-modern values and societies. However, from a different viewpoint religion can be both radical (that is, making fundamental change) and 'backward-looking'. For example, Islam in Iran was a source of opposition to the westernisation of the country under the Shah that ultimately brought about a revolutionary change to overthrow him. Yet the Islamic regime introduced policies that in some ways aimed to 'turn the clock back' to an earlier kind of social structure.

Another difficulty in identifying the role of religion in social change is that change is rarely the result of a single factor. As we saw earlier, Weber recognised the role of many different variables, not just religion, in bringing about capitalism. This being the case, it is not easy to separate out the particular contribution of religion to any given change. It may also be that, with secularisation, religion's ability either to promote change or to stand in its way have both been reduced. Weber would argue that behaviour is governed increasingly by the rational pursuit of secular goals rather than spiritual goals such as salvation.

To conclude, therefore, religion can act as a powerful force for social change, as Weber's argument for the role of Calvinism suggests. Equally, though, it can act as a conservative force to prevent change. However, it would be better to pose the question differently, to ask under what circumstances religion acts to bring about change or to prevent change. To answer this question, we would need to look closely at a range of factors.

These include the nature of the beliefs (e.g. do they encourage believers to act in new ways?), what groups they appeal to (e.g. the poor, the rich), and wider social, economic and political factors (e.g. are they colonial societies, how developed are they economically, are they already secularised?). If we have answers to some of these questions, we shall be in a better position to discover how far religion may bring about social change.

3 Ever since Troeltsch distinguished between church and sect, sociologists have been interested in ways of classifying and explaining different kinds of religious organisations and movements. There has been a particular interest in the more unusual minority or deviant types of religious organisation such as sects and cults. For example, sects can be seen as deviant since they reject mainstream society and its values and goals, and reject mainstream religion (i.e. churches) as too 'worldly' and corrupt, and even sometimes as the main enemy (the 'Antichrist'). Similarly, cults are often seen as deviant and as 'brainwashing' people into abandoning their family, education or career – though this may be more a media panic than a true picture, as Barker's study of the Moonies shows.

In recent decades, sociologists have noted the growth of new beliefs and groups that sometimes don't fit neatly into the old categories of sect, cult etc. These have been called 'new religious movements' and this has become a collective term used to cover the growing number of religious groups that have emerged since the 1960s and 1970s. (The media often refer to them as cults, though some sociologists would not use this label for all of them.) The term covers many different groups, such as Hare Krishna, Scientology, the Moonies, the Human Potential Movement (HPM) – which is a range of groups practising techniques for liberating members' potential – etc. Some draw on one or more religious traditions – usually Christianity and/or various eastern beliefs and practices such as Buddhism, Confucianism, yoga, etc. They vary in the degree of commitment expected of followers – from living in closed communities to simply attending a short course (e.g. TM – Transcendental Meditation). There are various ways of classifying them, such as which religion they are based on (though some like HPM aren't really based on any traditional religion), or how far they are in conflict with society. Roy Wallis has classified them into world-rejecting, world-accommodating and world-affirming movements.

Some writers regard these new movements as deviant – like the sects – and certainly they differ considerably from the 'normal' established churches such as Roman Catholicism or the Church of England. Eileen Barker estimates that there are now over 500 new religious movements in Great Britain. If so (and especially if they are in fact deviant), why have they become so popular?

Sociologists have put forward a number of different explanations for the growth of NRMs. Wallis identifies a number of social changes that he believes are responsible, especially because of their influence on the young. These include the longer and longer time spent in education, which lengthened the transition period from childhood to adulthood; the belief that technological progress would bring about the end of poverty and hunger; and the rise of radical political movements in the 1960s rejecting dominant values. World-rejecting NRMs seemed to offer a warmer, closer, more idealistic way of life and more loving relationships, which Bruce argues appealed to the young, especially after the failure of radical political movements and of hippie culture (as a result of drugs).

Others explain such movements in terms of deprivation or marginality. For example, Niebuhr argued that the traditional sect typically attracts members who are economically deprived and marginal to mainstream society – the poor, ethnic minorities, those with little education, etc. This echoes Weber's idea that sects offer the oppressed a sense of dignity and self-worth, e.g. telling them that they are the chosen ones, that they will be rewarded in the afterlife etc. (Weber calls this a theodicy of disprivilege – a religious explanation/justification of their suffering in this world.)

If this is true, we should expect NRMs to attract the poor – especially world-rejecting movements, since these are most likely to reflect the feelings of hostility towards wider society often held by deprived groups. However, Barker's study of the Moonies shows that the typical recruit was in fact more likely to be from a secure middle-class family background, so economic deprivation is clearly not the only reason for joining such movements. Barker found that the Moonies offered young adults warmth, support and a sense of community and commitment. It may be that relative deprivation – a subjective sense of lack, in this case a spiritual deprivation – rather than actual material deprivation is more important in explaining why young middle-class people are attracted to NRMs.

Wallis argues that world-affirming movements often develop after world-rejecting ones and they have tended to survive longer. They tend to recruit people of above-average income and education. World-affirming movements, such as TM and Insight, emphasise ways of gaining individual success in worldly terms (income, status etc.) and they enable those who are in fact already relatively successful to cope with a sense of inadequacy, or to re-discover their 'true selves' that they have lost sight of in the 'rat race'. Wallis links this type of movement to the conflict between a move towards a more leisure/consumption-oriented society and the traditional work ethic. Those who are most dedicated to their work (and successful in it) may be unable to enjoy leisure without feeling guilt, and such movements offer a guilt-free route to enjoyment of leisure.

Others such as Bruce argue that world-affirming movements are the result of the growing rationalisation (an idea based on Weber's views) and fragmentation of modern life. For example, work for most people has little meaning (it is not a vocation or calling) and doesn't provide a source of identity. Nor does it provide a sense of community – as Goldthorpe and Lockwood argue, workers are taking a more privatised orientation to work. However, people have been socialised to value achievement, but may lack the opportunity to do so. World-affirming movements offer followers techniques (such as meditation) to achieve both success and a spiritual dimension to modern life.

An alternative explanation for the growth of NRMs is the impact of dislocation and social unrest. Many sociologists argue that modern society is characterised by change and upheaval and that this causes dislocation or social disintegration. Changes result from processes such as industrialisation, modernisation, technological change and the upheavals this produces (e.g. redundancies, decline of traditional industries), the loss of support as a result of the decline of community and of the extended family. There is also a multiplication of belief systems, so that none of them appears authoritative any longer, and traditional religions fail to give a clear lead or guidance on how to live. In these situations, NRMs offer a solution to some people, providing a sense of certainty, community and identity. This approach draws on both Durkheim's idea of anomie – loss of norms or meaning, often resulting from rapid changes – and Weber's idea of rationalisation/bureaucratisation discussed above.

However, this view can be criticised. For example, Melton studied the founding of over 800 NRMs in the USA during the 20th century. Contrary to the view that they are a response to dislocation, he found that very many were founded in periods of stability such as the 1950s, not just at times of upheaval such as the 1960s and 1970s.

Bruce and others have suggested that the growth of NRMs is a result of secularisation – the decline in the influence of religious institutions, beliefs and practices in society. We have moved from a situation in the Middle Ages where one church had a monopoly, to one where more and more diversity (religious pluralism) is tolerated. In today's society, beliefs have become more watered down and people are less likely to make strong commitments. This has led to the decline of traditional sects, the rise of denominations and, more recently, of cults – much looser organisations that require fewer sacrifices and less commitment (e.g. to a particular creed),

which are thus more acceptable to modern 'customers'. This links to postmodernist ideas about pick 'n' mix cultures and identities. Institutions have less power to shape individuals' identities, and we can now 'shop around' and blend together elements of different beliefs and practices to suit our needs. This helps to explain the 'eclectic' (inconsistent, mixed) nature of beliefs like the Moonies, drawing on the bible, spiritualism, Confucianism etc. Similarly, Wilson argues that the growth of NRMs is evidence of secularisation – mainstream religious institutions and traditional beliefs are unable to attract and hold those searching for explanations and community.

Clearly, there is no single explanation of NRMs. This is not surprising, since the movements themselves are very diverse, so it would be surprising to find a single theory that explained them all. However, their recent and rapid growth suggests that they are bound up with other features of modern or 'postmodern' society, whether this is secularisation, rapid change, the loss of meaning, the shift to leisure and consumption, or growing individualism and the weakening of institutions.

Examiner's comment
This answer demonstrates a **good knowledge** of material, both **theoretical and empirical**, on new religious movements. The discussion is located in the context of a number of theoretical ideas about religion and society, such as rationalisation, social change, anomie, secularisation, etc. Different **classification systems** are presented for analysing religious movements, such as Troeltsch and Wallis, and there are plenty of **examples** of different movements. But rather than drifting off into a lengthy account of different types of NRMs, the answer remains focused on the set question, namely explaining their **growth**.
A range of different explanations and ideas (e.g. from Wallis, Bruce, Niebuhr, Weber, Wilson) are offered and several of these are well **evaluated** (e.g. using Melton, Barker).
A brief but **focused conclusion** pulls some key strands of the answer together.

How to score full marks

1 (a) One reason why urban growth doesn't always bring economic development is that often Third World towns and cities grow simply as a result of people escaping the poor conditions in the countryside. This 'surplus rural population' may migrate to the city because of things like land shortages in rural areas, famine, civil war and persecution. As a result, the town's population swells and its resources may be drained. This can happen especially if the influx is sudden, but also because the newcomers are less likely to be skilled, are often illiterate etc., so are often unable to contribute much to the urban economy anyway.

Another reason is to do with the role of many Third World cities as sub-metropolises helping to exploit their rural satellite territories on behalf of a capitalist metropolis overseas. For example, under colonialism many Third World cities were (and often still are today) just mechanisms for sucking out the country's resources. They were often port cities, and their function was to channel raw materials out of the hinterland and export them for manufacturing and processing in countries like Britain, France etc. So as they grew bigger, they actually helped not to develop the country, but to under-develop it.

> **Examiner's comment**
> **Two reasons** clearly identified as to why urban growth does not always bring development: the fact that it is often just an influx of displaced or impoverished peasants with little to contribute to growth, and the role of colonial cities in exploiting the colonies. Both of these are well explained, with good use of concepts (e.g. surplus rural population, metropolis/satellite).

(b) Some people argue that there is a 'population time bomb' and that high growth rates will destroy any chance of world development. However, there are several ways that population and development can be related. Firstly, population growth can in fact be a stimulus to development, as Item A says. A growing population can provide a growing market for goods, stimulating economic growth. In 19th-century Britain, an expanding population created a market for the goods produced by industrialisation. It can also provide a growing labour force, so that there is a workforce to enable development to occur. For Marxists, labour is the key factor in production, so the size of the population is important in economic growth.

Functionalists such as Durkheim also see population growth as important. He argues that a dense population is needed for the division of labour to develop, and this gives rise to specialisation and higher productivity. In some regions of Africa, sparsely populated areas have difficulty in developing.

Another relationship between population and development is that under-development can stimulate population growth. If a country has no welfare system, people often choose to have large families as a means of ensuring that someone will support them when they are old. Also, poverty generally means high death rates among children, so people have more children as insurance against some of them dying. From this point of view, under-development is the cause of population explosions. On the other hand, high population growth can also be caused by development – e.g. the success of modern healthcare systems and greater prosperity in reducing death rates – means that more survive and population expands. However, in general the more developed countries tend to have the lowest rates of population growth – in Europe they are now below replacement rates and population numbers may begin to decline.

Thus the relationship between population and development is complex. Population growth can be a stimulus to growth, not just an obstacle as is often thought, but under-development also may produce high rates of population growth.

> **Examiner's comment**
> A very good answer. As the conclusion recognises, the relationship between development and population is a complex one. Several views about the **links between the two** are examined and explained clearly.

2 Dependency theory, sometimes called under-development theory or neo-Marxism, was developed by Andre Gunnar Frank and others from the 1960s, partly in response to the modernisation theory. Frank sees Third World societies/economies as part of the global structure of capitalism. This system dominates its individual parts. Its basic feature is a chain of metropolis–satellite relationships. At one extreme is the global metropolis, the USA. This is linked ultimately to the poorest of the poor, the Third World landless labourer, via a chain of intermediate units that are both satellites and sub-metropolises (e.g. Third World capital cities). The system works by each level exploiting the one below it.

No real development is possible for the satellites within this system. In fact, Frank argues that since the system came into being with European expansion in the 16th century, the West has actively under-developed the Third World, i.e. distorted or blocked its development. He refers to this as the 'development of under-development' to emphasise that 'under-developed' is not the same as 'undeveloped' or 'traditional'. While these societies may have been undeveloped before they came under Western domination, this domination has changed them for the worse through exploitation, i.e. it has under-developed them.

Foster-Carter summarises dependency theory as being externalist, bilinear, stagnationist and discontinuist. Externalism means that factors outside the Third World dictate its development (or lack of). Bilinear means that satellites and the metropolis follow different courses – the satellites do not/cannot follow the same road to development already taken by the metropolis. Stagnationism means that the basic system never changes – the satellites remain trapped in under-development. Discontinuist means that to develop, the satellites will have to break their links with imperialism and the world capitalist system. For example, industrialisation in Latin America occurred largely during the two world wars when American and European influence there was weakened temporarily.

Dependency theory has had a huge impact on thinking about development. It is valuable in drawing attention to important issues such as the role of force and exploitation, the absence of a 'traditional' stage in many Third World societies. For example, Uruguay did not exist as a society before colonialism, while Inca and Aztec traditional societies were destroyed by force as the starting point for under-development. It is also valuable in emphasising the difficulties faced by Third World countries wanting to industrialise or break into markets already dominated by powerful Western multi-nationals. Because it focuses on the relationships between societies rather than just what occurs within a single country, it is able to show the importance of powerful external forces that shape a society's development prospects.

However, dependency theory has been subject to major criticisms both from the 'right' and the 'left'. Modernisation theory, in many ways its opposite (e.g. Foster-Carter summarises it as internalist, unilinear, recapitulationist and evolutionist), takes the basic view that to become more like 'us' (i.e. developed like the West), the Third World must become more like us (i.e. adopt Western values and institutions). This reflects modernisation theory's internalist view that the main obstacle to development lies within the Third World itself, in the form of 'traditional' cultures and social structures. For instance, the emphasis on ascribed status holds back economic development by preventing talented but low-born individuals from achieving.

Left-wing theorists have also attacked dependency theory on similar grounds, but they also argue that the weakness of Frank's theory is that it isn't sufficiently Marxist. For example, Bill Warren argues that internal aspects of Third World societies, especially their 'traditionalism', are more of an obstacle to development than external ones like imperialism. In fact, Warren sees imperialism as progressive, because it destroys such obstacles and clears the ground for capitalist development. Warren agues that this is a more Marxist view since – like Marx – it sees capitalism as progressive. This is not because capitalism is good in itself (Warren agrees that it is based on exploitation), but because it will bring into being a proletariat and hasten the socialist revolution on a world scale.

Warren also rejects Frank's view that capitalist development is not possible and argues that much has already taken place, especially since world war two. Similarly, while Frank sees nationalism as a valid political ideology that can justify breaking with the world system and thus aiding development, Warren regards it as completely negative and reactionary, preventing development.

While Warren's 'Marxist modernisation theory' is useful in pointing out some of the flaws in Frank's position – e.g. that some countries have achieved some development – this does not prove that all countries can develop. Other versions of dependency theory have taken this on board to some extent and argue that although some development opportunities occur, they are limited. The system itself remains in place, even if some countries can change their positions. For example, Wallerstein argues that as well as a core of capitalist states and a periphery of under-developed societies, there is a semi-periphery of partially developed societies, and that some (but not all) Third World countries can move into the semi-periphery. This also relates to the rise of the newly industrialised countries (NICs) such as South Korea and Singapore, which achieved rapid growth, especially in the 1980s and early 1990s. This may be a more useful version of dependency theory because it preserves the idea of structural inequality and exploitation, while allowing for the fact that some limited development does occur.

More recently, the trend towards globalisation – a single integrated world economy, and parallel trends in cultural and political spheres – has raised the question of whether dependency theory is correct. The answer depends to a large extent on how we interpret globalisation. Some see it as breaking down the power of Western states and multi-nationals to dominate the world economy, while others see it as strengthening the West. For example, the World Trade Organisation (WTO) prevents Third World countries from imposing protective tariffs to keep out the products of multi-national companies – whether to develop their own industries or to prevent ecologically damaging goods entering their markets. Dependency theorists would argue that this is just the most recent example of the power of the metropolis to impose itself on its satellites and stifle any competition, however limited, from Third World countries seeking to break out of the world system, or simply to improve their position within it. Thus, although dependency theory has been criticised on a number of grounds, it can to some extent be modified to take account of these criticisms, and it does serve to focus our attention on the massive inequalities of the global capitalist system within which (and against which) countries strive to develop.

Examiner's comments
This is a very good essay for several reasons. First of all, it shows a **sound knowledge and understanding** of a range of material – not only Frank's version of dependency theory, but Wallerstein's too, as well as modernisation theory and Warren's Marxist modernisation theory. Key concepts are **interpreted and used accurately**, such as metropolis/satellite, the development of under-development etc. The central features of dependency theory are **analysed** (e.g. its internalism, stagnationism), as are differences and similarities between the theories (e.g. both modernisation theory and Warren's Marxist version stress internal

obstacles to development). Dependency theory is **applied** to a number of situations (e.g. the NICs, the WTO) and **evaluated** via a number of different criticisms from other theories and in terms of different versions (e.g. Wallerstein's).

3 There are many differences between life in the developed countries of the West and life in the Third World, and one of the most important differences is in health and illness. People in the Third World are more likely to fall sick and, when they do, are less likely to get medical treatment (at least of the kind familiar in the West). Within many Third World societies there are also extreme inequalities of both health and healthcare, with the poor and rural populations having worse health and least access to healthcare.

On average, Third World people will also die younger than their Western counterparts. In the worst cases, such as parts of sub-Saharan Africa, life expectancy is barely half of the 75–80 years enjoyed in the West. The causes of death and illness also tend to be different. In the West, the main killers are degenerative diseases such as coronary heart disease, cancer and stroke, affecting older people. In many Third World countries, infectious diseases such as measles, TB, diphtheria, polio, cholera and malaria are major causes of death. Most of these greatly affect the young, and infant mortality is often 10 times higher than in the West. Recently, AIDS has become a major cause of sickness and death, with over two-thirds of all the cases (24 out of 35 million) in the world in sub-Saharan Africa. Again, this hits the younger, sexually active population more than the old. Because it hits young adults, this may have health and other effects on both the old and on children – two groups who young adults would normally be expected to provide and care for. However, as life expectancy increases, we are beginning to see more deaths from degenerative diseases.

One explanation of the ill health of Third World countries comes from modernisation theory. This is a functionalist-inspired theory that argues that if Third World countries want to develop, they must adopt the values, ideas and institutions of the West. As applied to health, this would involve adopting a rational scientific outlook on life and abandoning traditional and superstitious beliefs about the causes of illness. People in the Third World would need to give up traditional remedies and abandon traditional practices that may be causing illness. A good example of this is the ritual cannibalism practised in one New Guinea society, where the deceased's relatives ate his brains. It was found that this led to the spread of CJD in the population, and as more died from it their brains too were consumed, spreading the disease further. Other traditional practices, such as female circumcision, may also have adverse health effects. By abandoning such beliefs and practices in favour of scientific medicine and by educating people in the principles of hygiene, Third World health problems would be reduced. Modernisation theorists would also see the Western drugs companies as having a beneficial role, by spreading the necessary know-how to Third World countries so that they can tackle their health problems more effectively.

However, this view has been criticised as naïve by dependency theorists and others. For example, the big pharmaceutical companies that produce anti-AIDS drugs sell these at inflated prices that Third World countries cannot afford, and sometimes use Third World patients as the guinea pigs for drugs trials that might not be permitted in the West. Illich argues that Third World countries have become culturally dependent on the West, so that anything Western is seen as superior – in this case, Western medicine – thereby creating an insatiable demand for it. Similarly, much money is squandered on high-tech medicine and hospitals in the cities, when the real health needs of the rural poor are neglected. This reflects the fact that the decision-making elites live in the city.

Dependency theorists also criticise the 'modernisation' view for its similarity to the cultural model of illness, which blames the victim for their ill health (i.e. that illness is the result of their ignorance or superstitious beliefs). Dependency theorists favour a structural rather than cultural explanation. They argue that it is impossible to understand the health problems of the Third World without putting them in the context of the exploitation and under-development that the world capitalist system imposes on Third World countries.

One example of this view is Lesley Doyal. She argues that imperialism undermined the health of the peoples of East Africa. When the British established plantations for tea and other export crops in the 19th century, they found it impossible at first to get sufficient labour for them. They thus resorted to introducing a poll tax, which the native population had to pay. But as they lived in a cashless economy, the only way they could get money to pay the tax was by the men going to work for months at a time on the plantations. Men from many villages lived together in unhygienic conditions and infectious diseases spread rapidly. When they went home, they carried the diseases back to their families. A similar pattern exists today with the spread of AIDS in southern Africa, where men catch the disease when working in work camps at mines etc., then spread this throughout the region when they return home. Another recent factor is the increase in smoking throughout the Third World (at a time when it is in decline in the West). Multi-nationals can act without restrictions of the kind that exist in the West, and there is considerable evidence of dumping and smuggling of cigarettes by the tobacco industry to increase the addiction rate in Third World countries.

Dependency theorists thus have a different explanation of Third World illness, seeing it as caused by the structures of society and the relations between the West and the Third World created by under-development. The main problem is poverty, and Western medical techniques are unlikely to make much difference here. For example, even a relatively cheap method like mass vaccination of infants against measles often means that the child is saved from measles, only to die of some other infection, simply because poverty has weakened the immune system and squalid living conditions leave him or her constantly exposed to other diseases.

From this perspective the solution is therefore to tackle poverty and inequality, with the provision of things like clean drinking water, effective sanitation, adequate nutrition and social welfare generally being seen as more important than access to Western medicine. Providing these for the poor (the rich usually have them anyway) can make a major impact on health. For example, if we compare Sri Lanka and Brazil, we find that although Sri Lankans have an average income less than a fifth that of Brazilians, Sri Lanka has only a third of the infant mortality rate of Brazil. This is because Sri Lanka is a much more equal society, with more welfare provision for the poor. Tackling poverty is thus seen as the way to tackle ill health. This is similar to the West. As the Black Report and other studies show, illness is linked to poverty in Britain, and the way to reduce ill health and early death is to reduce social inequality.

Overall, then, we find a pattern of greater illness and more early death in Third World countries, often caused by infectious rather than degenerative diseases. While modernisation theorists see the solution in the spread of Western institutions and knowledge, dependency theorists reject this as naïve and argue that illness can only be explained in relation to poverty and exploitation resulting from world capitalism, and that health can only be improved by tackling these root causes, not by adoption of high-tech Western medicine. Of the two, from the evidence we have seen, dependency theory offers a more useful explanation of Third World health issues.

Examiner's comments
A very thorough answer that shows a good **knowledge of a range of theories and evidence**. It tackles the three issues raised by the question: both the **nature** and the **extent** of health problems, and the different solutions or **strategies** for dealing with them. It shows a good knowledge of the **patterns** of health and illness, causes of death etc. It **applies** modernisation and dependency theories very effectively to the question to create a basic framework to discuss explanations of these patterns and to evaluate possible strategies for improvement. There are lots of good **examples** and material from **studies** (e.g. on AIDS, CJD, health and imperialism, tobacco, comparative studies, the Black Report, drugs companies). It finishes with an effective summary of the main points to reach a reasoned **conclusion**.

How to score full marks

1 (a) Item B refers to the problem of not remembering to cover all the issues, but there are other drawbacks in not having a fixed set of precisely worded questions. A major one is that it might mean the interviewer asks different interviewees different questions, or the same question but with a different wording. The effect of this will be that you won't be able to make proper comparisons between their answers, as they weren't all 'exposed' to precisely the same question.

(b) Reliable data refers to data (i.e. results) that are reproducible by another researcher using the same method, sample etc. In other words, if a method produces reliable data, the second researcher will be able to repeat the first one's research and get the same results. It's often said that experiments, questionnaires and structured interviews tend to give reliable data.

Valid data refers to results that give a true or authentic picture of the thing being studied. For example, if a person understands your question and then answers it honestly, the data will be valid, whereas if they misunderstand or lie, you will get invalid data. It is said that unstructured interviews and PO give validity (though not reliability).

(c) One reason for choosing unstructured interviews is the sociologist's preferred perspective. Interactionists often prefer unstructured over structured interviews because they enable the researcher to examine closely people's meanings.

Secondly, they may use unstructured interviews in triangulation to provide qualitative data when the other method or source is a more quantitative one, such as data from a questionnaire or from official statistics.

Feminists often use unstructured interviews as they feel that the research process should be an equal one rather than the sociologist imposing his/her questions on the subject. Feminists believe that the outcome of research should be a joint collaboration between researcher and subject, and unstructured interviews allow the subject to speak about what she thinks is important, rather than having the sociologist set the agenda. Feminists also argue that because women are oppressed, a sensitive method such as unstructured interviews is essential in order to probe and explore this.

(d) One ethical problem is that for certain experiments to be successful, it may involve the researchers having to lie to the subjects (i.e. the people being experimented on). For example, after World War Two and the Nazi concentration camps, social scientists asked why were ordinary Germans willing to obey orders to murder people in this way. Stanley Milgram (a psychologist, not a sociologist) did an experiment in the 1950s in America to see how far ordinary Americans would go in obeying orders to harm others, if the orders came from someone in authority (in his experiment, a scientist in a white coat). The subjects were told they were involved in an experiment in learning, where the scientist told them to give an electric shock to the 'learner' every time he got a question wrong, even up to possibly fatally high voltages. In fact, the true aim was to see if they would obey authority. The 'learner' was an actor and there was no electric current, but if the subjects had known this (and that they were the real subject of the experiment not the 'learner'), the experiment would not have worked – i.e. it relied on deception.

A second ethical problem of using laboratory experiments is that they may actually do the subjects harm. This may have been the case with Milgram's experiments – the psychological stress of being pressured into apparently harming another person in the course of the experiment may have damaged some subjects. This could be an even greater risk with experiments on children, such as experiments that expose children to TV violence to study its effects on their behaviour (like Bandura).

2 There is a longstanding debate in sociology as to whether or not the subject can be considered to be scientific, and a wide range of arguments have been put forward both for and against the view. Early on in the development of sociology, in the late 19th century, a division emerged between the positivist view, that sociology could and should model itself on the natural sciences, such as physics, biology or chemistry, and on the other hand the interpretive view that the study of human society was fundamentally different to the study of the natural world and so required a radically different approach to that of the natural sciences.

For positivists such as Comte and Durkheim, the nature of society was no different from the nature of matter, and so both could be studied according to the same principles and methods, namely those that the positivists took to be characteristic of natural science. These were the observation of regularities or patterns in events (often through the use of controlled experiments), and the search for laws of cause and effect to explain these regularities. For example, if we drop an object, it falls to the ground at the same rate of acceleration every time. This can be measured and quantified, and then the physicist sets about searching for a law to explain this observed pattern (in this case, the law of gravity).

Durkheim argued that sociologists can and should follow this model. First of all we can observe in a detached way patterns or regularities (such as the suicide rate) and measure them quantitatively. Then we seek a causal explanation – for example that the suicide rate depends on the level of integration. Once we know the law governing the pattern (Durkheim argued that 'real laws are discoverable'), we can then predict future events, just as a physicist can predict what will happen when we drop an object.

The preferred method of the natural sciences is the laboratory experiment. However, there are practical problems with using this to study society – you can't fit a whole society into a lab. There may be ethical problems too, e.g. in trying to experiment on people to see if they will commit suicide. Instead, positivists use the comparative method, which parallels the experiment by finding two groups/societies that are alike except for one factor (e.g. their religion) and then seeing if this makes a difference to other patterns (e.g. the suicide rate). This way the cause can be identified, as in natural science.

Positivists like Durkheim also believed that, just as pure sciences like biology can explain how things like the human body work, applied sciences like medicine can use this knowledge to cure or prevent disease. Similarly, Durkheim believed that scientific sociology could discover the causes of social problems such as suicide, conflict etc., and that this would then point the way to their solution. Sociology would be able to tell society what policies to follow in order to 'cure' social 'ills'. Durkheim even uses medical terms like 'pathology' to describe these problems. He sums up this strategy by saying that the aim of sociology is 'to know, in order to predict, in order to control'.

Other sociologists have rejected positivism. Interpretivists (interactionists and ethnomethodologists) argue that human beings are not the same as matter. The key difference is that we have consciousness and free will or choice, so we don't simply react to a stimulus like physical objects do. Instead, we use our consciousness to interpret the meaning of a situation, and how we interpret it is what determines how we act. For example, if a child perceives the teacher's questioning as threatening, he/she may choose to retreat into silence, whereas if they interpret it as welcoming they are more likely to participate in class. Similarly, if we want to understand why a driver stops at a red light, we have to understand the meaning of 'red light' in that culture, i.e. how people interpret that particular symbol as meaning 'stop'. A naïve outsider (e.g. a visitor from Mars) might think that there was a cause and effect mechanism such as an automatic switch linking the red light to the car's brakes. In effect, this is the mistake positivists make when they look for causal laws of human behaviour – we don't work this way.

Anti-positivists therefore favour methods that give us access to people's meanings. The aim is what Weber called 'verstehen' or subjective understanding (empathy) – putting oneself in the place of the subject so as to see things as they do. Such methods of achieving verstehen include participant observation, unstructured interviews and life histories, and sources such as diaries, letters and other personal documents that give an insight into people's consciousness. This also means that we cannot study in a detached, 'scientific' way, as positivists argue, but must become involved with our subjects so as to understand their meanings.

Another criticism of positivism is that many sciences don't operate on a search for laws, but probabilities. Some also don't involve much use of laboratory experiments, such as astronomy or meteorology. Some writers distinguish between open and closed systems.

Before we can decide whether sociology is a science, we need to be clear what science is. However, there is also a debate about the nature of the natural sciences. According to Popper, its aim is not to discover laws since this is logically impossible (since the very next experiment might disprove it). Instead its aim is to try to refute (falsify) existing theories and in this way make progress – either by disproving a false theory, or by making us more confident in a theory by trying but failing to falsify it. This contrasts with the positivist view that real laws are discoverable and that they can be confirmed by the evidence.

An alternative view is Kuhn's notion of paradigms. This argues that there is not free-ranging debate within a science, but a paradigm or normative framework that determines what problems are worth investigating, what are acceptable methods, and even what answers should be found. The establishment of a single, shared paradigm means that scientists can stop debating the basics and get down to making progress in 'solving the puzzles' set by the paradigm. According to Kuhn, sociology has not yet established a single paradigm, but a series of competing 'schools' of thought that each see the basic issues of the subject differently. We can see this in the fundamentally different views of society held by positivists and interpretivists, or Marxists and functionalists. On this view, sociology might become a science in the future, but it is not one yet.

A related view to Kuhn's is the social construction view put forward by Knorr-Cetina, Mulkay, Woolgar and others. They argue that natural science does not study an objective reality, as positivists believe, but a socially constructed one. For example, to conduct any experiment involves accepting all sorts of 'knowledge-claims' as true without first testing them ourselves (e.g. that water boils at 100 degrees, that gravity is uniform). Similarly, materials, equipment etc. are not 'natural' but specially created for research purposes (e.g. laboratory mice are specially bred). So in fact the natural sciences are another example of how knowledge is socially constructed, rather than being 'pure' and somehow detached from society. This means it is perhaps not the ideal model that positivists take it to be. This view is similar to the postmodernist idea that all methodologies and epistemologies (theories of knowledge) are really just metanarratives – 'stories' (or opinions) that have been constructed, rather than 'the truth'.

Overall, whether we believe it is possible to describe sociology as a scientific discipline hinges on a number of issues. We would have to accept the positivist view that real laws of human society are discoverable (without being able to use experiments to establish them), rather than the interpretivist view that humans cannot be studied scientifically because we have consciousness and free will and so need to be studied using empathetic qualitative methods. It also depends on whether we accept that the natural sciences do in fact work as the positivists believe – a view challenged by more recent studies of how scientists work in practice.

3 Along with Durkheim and Weber, Marx is regarded as one of the key founders of modern sociology, and his ideas have had a huge impact on the development of the subject. Marx spent almost all his adult life in 19th-century Britain, which was becoming the world's first industrial capitalist power. Marx was also a political activist who sought to understand the workings of capitalism in order to overthrow it and replace it with a free and classless communist society. In analysing capitalism, Marx developed a range of concepts and theories that sociologists have tried to apply and develop in order to understand today's society.

A key principle for Marx is materialism. This is the idea that society is based on the fact that humans must engage in production to meet their needs. The form that production takes (e.g. the kind of technology) and the way it is organised (e.g. how labour is divided, and who owns/controls production), shape everything else about society – its institutions, ideas and beliefs. Sometimes this is called the base/superstructure model – the economy being the base, with all other features of society arising from it and shaped by it. It is also known as economic determinism – the idea that the economy determines every other aspect of society.

Related to this is the idea of conflict. According to Marx, all societies except the simplest (which he calls primitive communism), are based on a division into two classes – the owners of the means of production (factories, land etc.) and the non-owners (e.g. the serfs in feudalism, the proletariat or wage-slaves in capitalism). In every case, the owners exploit the labour of the non-owners. In capitalism, the bourgeoisie exploit the labour of the proletariat, extracting surplus value or profit from them. This results in class conflict and ultimately will give rise to the overthrow of the capitalism and its replacement with a communist, classless society in which the means of production will be owned collectively and used to satisfy human needs rather than produce profit. This will bring about the end of exploitation and alienation.

Meanwhile, however, capitalism is maintained, firstly by the power of the capitalist state (which Engels defined as an instrument for the centralisation of the means of oppression) – prisons, police, courts, armies etc. can be used to suppress opposition. Secondly, by means of bourgeois ideology – beliefs and ideas that justify the rule of the minority, often spread by the mass media, religion and the education system – the proletariat can be persuaded to accept capitalist rule. As a result of what Althusser calls the repressive state apparatus and the ideological state apparatus, therefore, the overthrow of capitalism has been postponed.

Marx's views have been widely criticised. Writers have argued against Marx's materialism and the base/superstructure model, that material factors do not always play a decisive role in society and that ideas can sometimes be more important. For example, Weber argued that it was religious ideas (specifically Calvinism) that brought about modern capitalism, not simply material developments in the economy. Many modern or neo-Marxists have also argued that the proletariat will never lead a revolution against capitalism until they have changed their consciousness (i.e. their ideas). However, Marx himself was aware that ideas/consciousness play a key role in bringing about change, although he also argued that the material conditions for change must first be present. Similarly, 20th-century Marxists like Gramsci argued that it was the struggle for hegemony or ideological leadership of society that determined which class would rule.

Another area of criticism is the predominant position that Marx gives to social class in his theory, and of his definition of class. He sees classes as groups of people who share the same relationship to the means of production as one another. For example, all workers belong to the same class because they are all non-owners who are exploited by the capitalists. This is a class in itself. When the members of a class become conscious of their shared position and true interests (e.g. in needing to overthrow the capitalists), Marx calls this a class for itself – i.e. one that understands and acts in its own interests.

However, critics argue that his model of class is too simplistic. Weberians argue that ownership/non-ownership is only one criterion of class and that both Marx's classes may actually contain several different classes. Of course, this depends on how class is defined – e.g. Weberians like Goldthorpe and Lockwood define it in terms of position in the labour market, thus giving skilled, unskilled, professional etc. classes. Weber also argued that class was not the only form of inequality or stratification and added power and status as other dimensions that may sometimes be more important than class. Marxists, however, respond by arguing that class generally underlies and ultimately determines these other forms of inequality, though this seems hard to prove. Feminists have also criticised Marxism for neglecting gender inequality and oppression or subordinating it to class. For instance, radical feminists argue that patriarchy, not class, was historically the first form of inequality, in which men exploited women.

While Weberians and feminists generally share Marxists' emphasis on conflict, functionalists see society as being based on shared values rather than class exploitation. They thus reject the Marxist view that conflict is inevitable so long as inequality exists and argue that inequality benefits everyone, not just those at the top, since it ensures that the most important roles are performed by the most talented people. Marxists, however, seem more realistic here, in rejecting the functionalist claim that we live in a meritocracy where this would be possible. Instead, Marxists such as Westergaard and Resler present detailed evidence of the inherited inequalities that exist in modern society.

A more important criticism comes from social action approaches such as interactionism. These argue against the view that we are simply 'puppets' of the social system or social structure, manipulated into meeting its needs. This criticism was originally aimed at functionalism by Dore, but it has also been applied to Marxism, since one version of Marxism (usually called structuralist Marxism) argues that everything in society (e.g. people's actions and consciousness, social institutions etc.) exist to serve the needs of capitalism. There is certainly some truth in this criticism, but it is also possible to find in Marx's own writing examples to contradict this. For example, he says 'men make their own history' – i.e. people can decide how to act, whether to try to change the world etc. – though he adds that they do so 'not in conditions of their own choosing' (i.e. the structure of capitalism imposes limits on what they can and cannot do at any one moment).

There are also variations within Marxism. For example, there is both structural Marxism on the one hand and a type of Marxism that borrows interpretive or interactionist ideas on the other. Gouldner makes a similar distinction between scientific Marxism and humanistic Marxism. A good example of a sociologist who combines both structural and interpretive aspects is Paul Willis. He uses interpretivist ideas and methods to investigate how working-class boys come to actively 'choose to fail' and happily end up in working-class jobs, which is what meets the 'system needs' of capitalism – i.e. they choose to occupy the roles that the structure requires. Although Willis has been criticised for his small-scale, unrepresentative study, he offers insights into how capitalism goes about reproducing itself through our actions.

In one way, most of what the later Marxists have written is an attempt to explain the shortcomings of some of Marx's original ideas. Especially, Marx had originally expected that a revolution to overthrow capitalism would occur in his own lifetime, but this did not happen. After his death, revolutions again failed to occur in the developed western countries where Marx had predicted they would begin. According to Perry Anderson, western Marxists were obliged to explain this, and most of them focused on the role of ideas and ideology as the main obstacle to the workers developing a revolutionary consciousness (rather than the material factors that Marx had put at the centre of his theory). As a result, many Marxists now seem more concerned with explaining how capitalism is maintained or reproduced rather than how it will be overthrown. We can also see that Marxist ideas have been combined with others (such as feminism) to try to make sense of the world. This suggests that Marxism on its own is inadequate as an explanation of society today.

Examiner's comments
A **sound knowledge and understanding of Marx's key ideas** – materialism, determinism, base and superstructure, class and class conflict, ideology, exploitation, revolution – and of **variations** within Marxism and combinations of Marxism with other approaches. The usefulness of such ideas is **evaluated** from various standpoints – Weberian, feminist, functionalist, interpretivist. The conclusion is interesting and well reasoned, and can be linked back both to the question and to the introduction. It's worth remembering that Marx's views have been interpreted and re-interpreted by countless writers, friend and foe alike – so any two accounts of Marxism are likely to pick up on different features of his ideas.

5 Crime and Deviance

🎯 How to score full marks

(a) One advantage of using participant observation as a way of studying crime and deviance is that the world of the deviant is often a closed one – since they are breaking rules, they do not make themselves readily available to study. Thus participant observation is very useful, especially if covert (i.e. where the subjects of the research don't know the investigator's true identity or purpose, but believe him/her to be one of the group). Covert PO allows the researcher to see things that would otherwise remain hidden to 'normal' or 'straight' society, such as Humphrey's study of homosexual activity in public toilets, or Ditton's study of pilfering among bread deliverymen. It could be said that it enables us to see how the other, deviant, half live.

One problem with using PO to study deviance is that, by being deeply involved with the deviants (which is necessary for the sociologist to gain a true understanding of them), the sociologist may become too sympathetic and lose his/her objectivity, thus producing a biased and distorted account of the group which sees them through rose-tinted spectacles.

(b) Although the concept of deviance is usually used mainly in the study of crime, it can be applied to more or less any area of social life. In this answer, I will look at how the concept can be used in studying three topics I am familiar with. These are education, work and leisure, and religion.

In education, interactionists such as Hargreaves and Becker have used the concept of deviance to explain educational failure. The school has norms and values – an ethos or culture – that it expects pupils to adhere to. However, some pupils are unable or unwilling to conform to these. This can often result from teachers labelling and stereotyping pupils on the basis of their background (e.g. seeing black boys as troublesome). Pupils may then internalise the label and live up to it. If the label is a deviant one, a self-fulfilling prophecy has been created and the pupil becomes what the label predicts he/she will be – disruptive and uncooperative. As a result, he/she may fail. Deviant, anti-school subcultures may be formed by those who the school has defined as failures. As in other deviant subcultures (e.g. those studied by Albert Cohen), members may have failed in terms of mainstream goals and so seek status in the alternative hierarchy offered by the deviant group. They do this by inverting the school's values – e.g. the school values regular, punctual attendance, so the anti-school subculture rewards those who truant.

The concept of deviance can also be applied to work and leisure. Some views of leisure, especially of working-class youth, see deviance as a solution to the problem of boredom and exclusion. Working-class male adolescents have few resources (e.g. no income) and time on their hands. One solution to the boredom this produces is deviant behaviour, to bring excitement to their lives. Similarly, Miller argues that lower-class subculture values toughness (e.g. pub brawls) which tends to lead to deviant behaviour. Likewise, behaviour in work often involves deviance – such as pilfering or white-collar crime. According to Sutherland, differential association normalises criminal behaviour at work for those who engage in it (e.g. workers say it's OK to steal from the employer or client 'because everyone's at it').

Lastly we can look at religion. Troeltsch classified religious organisations into church and sect – church being mainstream, upholding the status quo, and sects being radical and opposed to mainstream society and its values, and hence deviant. As in Merton's typology, sects are like Merton's 'rebels', since they reject mainstream values but substitute their own radical (in religious terms) values. A lot of new religious movements, such as the Moonies, the Jesus Army, Jonestown, Solar Temple etc., are seen as deviant, practising strange rituals, deviant sexual behaviour (e.g. group marriage), brainwashing members into abandoning 'normal life', family and career etc. The very terms 'nonconformist' (used to describe Protestants who dissented from the Church of England) and 'unorthodox' were originally used to describe religious deviance and show that the concept is not confined to crime, but can be applied to religious movements. Durkheim focused on the consensus role of religion, but consensus is sometimes reinforced by persecuting those who disagree with mainstream beliefs (as in witch-hunts) as deviants.

(c) Marxist theories often focus on power in their explanations of crime and deviance. This derives first from Marx's emphasis on the material base of society and the idea that all power – political, judicial etc. – derives from economic sources, and secondly from Marx's writing on crime itself, where he sees most crime as deriving from the poverty caused by capitalism. For example, the slogan '(private) property is theft' sums up the basic view of traditional Marxist criminologists. That is, they ask the questions: 'what is really criminal (in the widest sense of the term)' and 'is it this that the judicial system punishes?' Their answers are that capitalism is itself a crime against society, and that the judicial system doesn't punish capitalism. This is because the capitalist class possesses the power to avoid punishment, and to punish others.

Marxists thus tend to focus on the crimes of the powerful. Chambliss' study of Seattle found that much of the crime was committed by an extensive crime syndicate. This group embraced members of the business community, the police, the coroner's office, and other individuals of high status, power and influence. Its members were connected by blood, marriage and shared interest. Chambliss found that the police did nothing to stop the group's serious, wide-ranging criminal activities, but instead focused on working-class crime. Chambliss focuses on the differential enforcement of the law and the ability of the powerful to evade investigation, prosecution or conviction. Similarly, Carson found that breaches of health and safety regulations by factory owners were rarely prosecuted, and that when they were, the fines imposed were derisory.

We can add that Marxists argue that not just law enforcement, but also law-making is biased in favour of the powerful – the ruling class make laws in their own interest. For example, squatting (by powerless homeless people) is often criminalised, whereas owning two or more homes (by the rich and powerful) is not a crime. The laws uphold the rights of those with power, rather than those of the poor.

These traditional Marxist studies have been both criticised and updated by the work of theorists who are usually described as neo-Marxists or critical criminologists. Among these are Taylor, Walton and Young, whose book 'The New Criminology' has been one of the most influential in this field. They combined a Marxist analysis of modern capitalist society with some of the key ideas of labelling theory. They took a libertarian, non-judgemental stance towards deviance (unlike traditional functionalist criminology). They maintained that criminologists must examine the socio-economic structure within which crime takes place, as well as, at the micro level, the interaction processes of negotiation and labelling (e.g. between police and suspect) that go towards

'criminalising' an individual. They recognise that crime may be politically motivated (an idea that has some similarity with Merton's category of rebellion), discussing the Black Panthers, the Gay Liberation Front and others who have broken the law in pursuit of a political cause. They also put forward the idea that a poor person stealing from a rich person commits a 'Robin Hood' act that is instrumental in changing society. However, it is not clear how an act that has an economic motive (i.e. personal gain) can bring political change.

The New Criminologists thus draw on the insights of the interpretivists (such as interactionists, phenomenologists), who observe that only when an act is labelled as deviant does it become deviant. In other words, it involves the power of some people to impose a label usually regarded as negative and very undesirable on other people. There is no absolute measure and therefore the sociologist's task is to document the process by which a label is imposed, adopted and sustained through interactions (e.g. between the labelled and the police, employers, neighbours etc.). While labelling theorists do deal with issues of power, they have been criticised for focusing excessively on the micro level and on the role of 'middle range officials' such as the police, probation officers, social workers, psychiatrists and teachers. These people impose the labels, thereby neglecting the wider structures of inequality from which, Marxists argue, the labels originate. Nevertheless, their contribution is valuable in showing the processes by which an act and an actor become labelled.

Stuart Hall, another neo-Marxist, has combined Marxist and interactionist ideas to explain the moral panic about mugging that occurred in the 1970s. He claims that British capitalism was undergoing a crisis of hegemony at this time. Student protests against the Vietnam War, miners' and other strikes and growing unrest meant that the ruling class were finding that popular consent to their exercise of power was being undermined. Hall argues that the media-led panic about young black men committing violent street robberies at this time was a direct response, not to actual events (there was no evidence of a real increase in the crime), but to this crisis of hegemony and the need of capitalism to stabilise its rule. Hall sees the moral panic about mugging and the scapegoating of black youth as a way for the ruling class to legitimise a general strengthening of 'law and order' and to win consent for a more repressive stance. Thus he sees both the way crime is defined (there was no defined crime of 'mugging' at the time), and which crimes the police, media etc. focus on, as being inextricably linked to the needs of the powerful.

'New Left Realists', including leading former New Criminologists such as Jock Young, have been critical of Marxist, neo-Marxist and New Criminology accounts of crime and deviance. They criticise the emphasis that these approaches place on the crimes of the powerful, pointing out that most working-class crime is against other members of the working class and that so-called 'Robin Hood' crimes do not dislodge the rich from their position of power. New Left Realists highlight what Young calls multiple aetiology – multiple and related causes of crime – and reject New Criminology's sympathy for the offender, pointing out that victims must be studied too and are often the most vulnerable in society. In their consideration of offenders, they focus much less on definitions of deviance, and far more on ideas of subculture and relative deprivation, although marginality can be seen as linked to lack of power. They see improvements in policing as important and Kinsey, Lea and Young warn against 'military style' policing. While they see power as important, they see it as far from the only factor.

Marxists have been criticised for their preoccupation with class and economic crime, and feminists have highlighted the importance of gender and power for a full understanding of crime. They see women's relative power as crucial. Freda Adler has proposed the theory that women's liberation (and thus presumably greater female power) has led to greater levels of female crime. Heidensohn too sees power as important – but she sees the still low number of female criminals as caused by social control of women which, through demands on their time in the home and on their 'reputation' outside of it, gives them little chance to commit crimes.

In conclusion, it seems clear that the idea of power is central to an understanding of crime and deviance. After all, deviance can only exist if someone has the power to make and enforce rules. It is obvious that any approach that examines rule-breaking and disorder has to have some notion of power – even consensus approaches have to explain who has the power to deal with such problems and where this power comes from. However, this essay has concentrated mainly on theories that focus on conflict, because these approaches seem to have most to say about the power to make and enforce rules, and in whose interests it is to define certain groups as deviant or criminal.

How to score full marks

(a) There are many problems in trying to use occupation to measure class. Firstly, not everyone has an occupation. The unemployed, full-time students, pensioners, the disabled etc. are all without paid work, so to classify these people we have to 'attach' them to someone who does have a job, e.g. students could be put in their parents' class. One problem here is that for example a working-class university student may have much better future job prospects than their parents. Alternatively, we could use the last occupation that pensioners, the unemployed etc. had – but this might have been a higher income level than they now enjoy, so it would give an invalid picture of their current class position.

A big problem for occupational measures is the 'unit of analysis'. This means do we use families/households, or individuals within them? When only men did paid work, it was reasonable to put the whole household in the class to which his occupation belonged, but nowadays most women work too, so feminists argue that they should be put into a separate class from their husbands. Similarly, if they are the main breadwinner (as they are in many households), it might make more sense to classify the husband according to his wife's job and not vice versa.

Occupational measures also ignore the very wealthy who do not need to work because they own huge amounts of property and live off their investments. This 'invisible' class may be very small, but Marxists argue that it is the ruling class of super-rich capitalists, and that their wealth and power give the class structure its shape and direction. Thus feminists, Marxists and others identify problems in using occupation to measure class.

(b) Many sociologists have seen class as the key feature of modern society. As Item A notes, occupational class is the backbone of the stratification system, affecting lifestyle, life-chances, political outlook and status.

For example, in studying education it was clear that a pupil's social class has a major influence on their chances of success, for several reasons. Firstly, class position affects a family's wealth, so middle-class parents can give material support to their children to improve their chances of educational success. Within school, teachers may stereotype pupils because of their class background, for example seeing working-class children as lazy or uncooperative. As a result, they may devote less time to them and such children may fail to progress, thereby fulfilling the teacher's low expectations of them. However, not all working-class pupils fail and many have very supportive parents and teachers.

Class may also affect political beliefs and voting behaviour. Traditionally, most working-class voters supported Labour and the middle class voted Conservative. However, there have always been 'deviant' voters and writers such as Crewe argue that there has been a class de-alignment. Furthermore, it may not be class, but particular features of certain groups that affects their political behaviour – e.g. Labour voting is linked with manual workers (i.e. class), but even more with union membership, working in the public sector, living in the north, council house tenure etc. This raises the problem of defining class – e.g. unskilled manual workers have a different market situation, compared to skilled workers. Should we treat them as one class or two? If unskilled workers' life-chances, values etc. are different from skilled workers, then perhaps we have to say they are in different classes. If so, the argument is circular, as we are defining class by its effects.

Another major area where class affects our lives is health. This is an aspect of life-chances, because it is about how likely different groups are to enjoy a long and healthy life. Male manual workers are about three times more likely to die before retirement than professional males, and working-class people are more likely to suffer disabilities, chronic illness and death from almost all causes compared to middle-class people. Marxists argue that this is due to their structural position within capitalism – poverty and low pay, exploitation and the stress it creates, industrial injuries and diseases undermine working-class health. However, it could also be due to the distinctive subcultural values held by the lower working class, of short-term hedonism with little thought for the future health consequences of their lifestyle, such as drinking and smoking.

However, although most sociologists would argue that class has a major influence on our lives, other factors such as gender, ethnicity and age are also important. Some sociologists, influenced by postmodernism, would also argue that the influence of class is declining. For example, as overall living standards improve, the absolute poverty experienced in the past by many unskilled workers is disappearing. Likewise, although there are still health inequalities, manual workers today live longer than professionals of two or three generations ago, and the number of babies of any class that die in their first year is now very small indeed.

Nevertheless, class remains an important factor in health, education, politics and elsewhere.

(c) Stratification is the ranking of different groups or individuals in terms of rewards, such as power, status or wealth. The view that stratification is both inevitable and beneficial to individuals and society is associated with the functionalist view. Functionalists believe that society is a system of interdependent parts, the function of each part being to meet the needs of the social system to achieve its goals and maintain itself. Functionalists therefore approach any aspect of society from the point of view of how it meets the system's needs and fits with other parts of that system.

This can therefore be applied to the study of stratification. As with anything else – such as the family, religion etc. – functionalists seek to identify the functions that stratification performs. According to Parsons, an important function of stratification is that it provides an incentive for the most able to take on the most important roles that society needs to have fulfilled. Exactly which positions these are will depend on the value system of that society. For example, modern society greatly values the accumulation of wealth, so the key roles will include those of wealth-creating entrepreneurs. By contrast, traditional North American Indian societies valued bravery in war and skill in hunting, and so they rewarded most highly those who showed these qualities. As a functionalist, Parsons believes in a value consensus, i.e. that these values are shared by the whole of society – whose members are thus united in agreeing what qualities deserve rewarding.

Davis and Moore apply this approach to modern industrial society. In order to place the most able people in the most important roles, society offers high rewards. This motivates everyone to strive for these positions. Secondly, society has a meritocratic structure, i.e. it selects people on the basis of their achievements and ability, not on the basis of ascribed characteristics such as class background, skin colour etc. This fits with Parsons' view that modern society is characterised by a set of norms that are individualistic, achievement-oriented and universalistic – i.e. we get our positions as

individuals (not as a group), through our own efforts (not through birth) and according to a set of rules that are applied equally to everyone, like in an examination (not 'one rule for the rich').

So we have an open competition, especially through the education system – all have an equal chance and are equally motivated to do well, and the best win through to get the highest rewards. The losers have to settle for lower rewards, but they too gain from the fact that key roles are performed by the most able people. For example, they will be treated by competent doctors who got there through ability, rather than by incompetent ones who got there through favouritism. Thus stratification is both inevitable and beneficial – inevitable because individuals are, according to functionalists, unequal in their abilities, and beneficial because it enables society to select the most able for the most socially valued roles.

The functionalist view has been widely criticised, however. Marxists in particular have criticised the view that stratification is inevitable. Marx argued that inequality is characteristic of certain phases of the development of society, but that in its earliest form, there was equality based on extreme scarcity, and that following the overthrow of capitalism, an equal, classless, communist society based on abundance will come into being. However, both the Marxist and the functionalist view are making untested statements about the future – we cannot logically know whether society will always remain unequal or whether it will one day become equal.

Nevertheless, it could be argued that no society has managed to create full equality between its members. Attempts to do so have generally not lasted very long, such as the former Soviet Union, while the Israeli kibbutzim are said to be increasingly unpopular (even if we accept that they may have achieved greater equality than is found in the wider Israeli society). This evidence seems to lend some support to the functionalist view of the inevitability of stratification.

Another problem with the functionalist view is that it rests on the idea of meritocracy. For example, society can only benefit from the most able performing the most important jobs if in fact the most able get the chance to compete for these positions. But in many societies, meritocracy does not exist. Functionalists recognise this to be true in traditional, pre-industrial societies, where positions are allocated on the basis of ascribed characteristics – e.g. leaders are usually simply the sons of leaders, not necessarily the bravest, cleverest etc. individuals. (This can be seen in the case of hereditary monarchies.) Critics would argue that it is also true in modern industrial societies – for example, much research into education shows that working class, black and other groups are disadvantaged (e.g. by teachers labelling these pupils as 'thick'), so able pupils from poor backgrounds get fewer opportunities than those from wealthier backgrounds. If so, the most important roles will not be fulfilled by those most able to perform them, and society as a whole will suffer. In the earlier example, students may get into medical school because their parents are doctors, not because they have the most aptitude for the job.

This also raises the problem of how we identify the most important jobs. For functionalists, the shared value system tells us what a society believes is important, but critics argue that there is no shared value system. For example, different social classes have different values and see different jobs as important, with middle-class people ranking jobs according to their perceived high status (such as accountants), whereas manual workers rank jobs according to their perceived usefulness (such as sewage workers). According to Davis and Moore, jobs can be ranked according to their skill (the amount of training needed to do them) and the authority they have over others. But it is hard to compare skill levels objectively (women's jobs often get ranked as less skilled simply because they are done by women!), and whether a job has authority over others may be a matter of custom rather than necessity – e.g. doctors have more power over nurses than over midwives, yet nurse and midwife training is essentially similar.

A major plank in the functionalist argument is that inequality is beneficial to everyone – a view shared by the New Right. This view argues that inequality benefits both rich and poor. If the rich are not taxed heavily and are encouraged to invest and expand their businesses, this will create jobs and incomes for the poor. (This is called 'trickle down economics' – some of the wealth created flows down from the rich to the poor.) By contrast, if the state tries to impose equality by taxing the rich heavily, this just discourages them from investing, the economy declines and poverty increases for all. In any case, in the age of globalisation, the wealthy can just export their capital to low-tax countries, so according to this argument it's not even worth trying to reduce inequality.

However, this view assumes that rich and poor share the same interests. Conflict theorists disagree. They see the relationship between the classes as a 'zero sum' – one gains at the expense of the other. For Marxists, capitalists are rich because the proletariat are poor, and the view that stratification is inevitable and beneficial is simply an ideology to justify exploitation and conceal the fact that the bourgeoisie benefit at the proletariat's expense.

Thus it cannot easily be said that stratification is both inevitable and beneficial to individuals and society. Inevitability is perhaps impossible to demonstrate logically (since we cannot know how things will be in the future). Clearly it is beneficial to some – those at the top of the system. Whether we accept that it benefits those lower down, e.g. by ensuring that the most talented individuals perform the most important jobs for the benefit of all, depends on whether we accept, firstly, that there is a meritocracy in place to enable the talented to reach the top and, secondly, on whether we accept that those at the top use their position to benefit society as a whole or – as conflict theorists would argue – merely to benefit themselves.

Examiner's comment
A well-organised answer that **tackles all the key aspects** of the question. It looks both at whether stratification is **inevitable** and whether it is beneficial, and at who benefits from it. The answer has a good analytical structure – points are explained and developed, and their importance drawn out very clearly, and it has a conclusion that is firmly based on what has been discussed in the main body. It shows a very good **knowledge and understanding** of relevant sociological views, including functionalism, Marxism and the New Right, and uses relevant evidence (e.g. on the former Soviet Union, class differences in ranking of occupations) – although a little more empirical evidence from studies of stratification would be welcome, and it could also bring in a feminist view on whether gender stratification is inevitable and beneficial. There is some very good evaluation throughout the answer of the different views put forward – especially of functionalism, but also of other approaches too.